CW00950109

A life too soon done

Sheffield General Cemetery and The Great War

Shirley Baxter and Hilary McAra

Original research by Nancy Greenwood

The Sheffield General Cemetery Trust

Written by Shirley Baxter and Hilary McAra supported by Nancy Greenwood, Jo Meredith and Alex Quant.

Printed by People for Print Ltd.

ISBN 978 0953999460

Whilst every effort has been made to check the accuracy of information, we can not guarantee that there are no errors in the content of this book.

Acknowledgements

LOTTERY FUNDED

This project was entirely funded through the Heritage Lottery Fund First World War then and now programme

The Sheffield General Cemetery Trust gratefully acknowledges the Sheffield City Council Archive and Local Studies Service for their support over many years. We would also like to thank the following organisations and people:

National Archives, the Imperial War Museum, York and Lancaster Museum, the National Coal Mining Museum, Veterans Affairs, Canada, Sheffield Hallam University, the families of the servicemen who have contributed information and photographs, and all the volunteers and members of the local community who contributed to the project.

'To us it seemed his life was too soon done
Ended, indeed, whilst scarcely yet begun'

Memorial Inscription for Frederick Ashton who is buried in
Sheffield General Cemetery

Contents

List of Illustrations

Front Cover: World War One campaign medals

Images are from the Sheffield General Cemetery Trust (SGCT), Picture Sheffield at Sheffield Libraries, Ancestry.co.uk, The Imperial War Museum collection (IWM), Wikipedia, Sheffield Cathedral, Sheffield Hallam University or reproduced with permission from the serviceman's family or the person named.

7

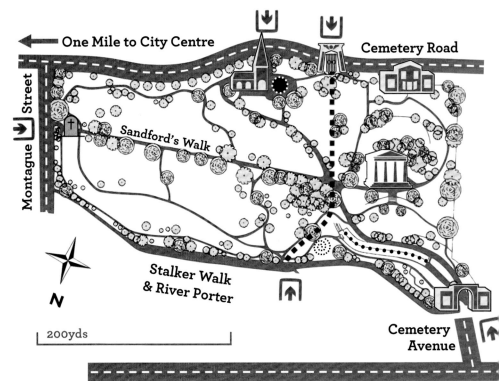

One Mile to City Centre

Cemetery Road

Sandford's Walk

Stalker Walk
& River Porter

N

200yds

Cemetery
Avenue

One Mile to City Centre

Ecclesall Road, S11

 Nonconformist Chapel

War Memorial

 Anglican Chapel

Gatehouse

 Egyptian Gate

Original Cemetery Office

Geological Stone Spiral

Dissenters' Wall

 Catacombs

Entrance

Sheffield General Cemetery

Preface

Sheffield General Cemetery is hidden away behind Ecclesall Road in the city's western suburbs. Originally opened in 1836, this historic Victorian landscape is now enjoyed as a local park whilst still being the resting place for over 87,000 burials.

This book traces the stories of some of the 111 servicemen of the First World War, the majority from Sheffield, who are buried or commemorated in the Cemetery. The names of the 30 men buried in the Cemetery can be seen on the War Memorial erected and maintained by the Commonwealth War Graves Commission (CWGC) near the Montague Street entrance. The names of those who were buried or commemorated where they fought and died were only recorded in the Cemetery on family grave stones, many of which were removed when the Cemetery landscape was restored in 1980. Although the stones may have been removed, their locations and inscriptions are all recorded in the Cemetery burial records.

Information for this book was taken from those records and, where available, from monumental inscriptions on family grave stones. This was followed by a search of the CWGC website and any surviving military service records on the websites findmypast.co.uk and ancestry.co.uk. The National Archives, the British Newspaper Archive and Forces War Records were also consulted. An individual's name is often recorded differently in the different documents, which is why more than one spelling is given for some of the names in this book.

The starting point for anyone researching a soldier who died in the First World War is the Commonwealth War Graves Commission (CWGC) website. The Imperial War Graves Commission was established in 1917 to record the details of every man or woman who died as a result of armed conflict. Now the Commonwealth War Graves Commission honours the memory of 1,700,000 men and women who died in two world wars and ensures that they are never forgotten.

Some military records are available online but the vast majority were destroyed by fire in the Second World War, so to come upon a soldier's records is a great find. Where they exist, they can be very detailed and the record keeping is impressive. Occasionally medical records and/or pension records are available. It is usually possible to find a serviceman's medal index card and occasionally local newspapers contain information. War diaries contain detailed descriptions of each day's action and can be useful, particularly if researching an officer.

This book gives details for all the men buried in the Cemetery and for a representative sample of the commemorated men. The index lists the names and military details of all the men and their respective burial plots. Further information is kept in the Cemetery records.

As we started our research we discovered that there were many terms about which we were unsure and so we thought it would be helpful if we were to write a brief explanation of some of these at the beginning of the book to help readers fully understand the lives of the Servicemen we are discussing. We do not pretend to be World War One historians, but we have learnt a lot, and we would like to share our knowledge to help us all fully appreciate the sacrifice of these brave men.

We are aware that many women served their country in the First World War, but as all those buried or commemorated in the Sheffield General Cemetery are men, we use the male pronoun.

Background to the War

The Structure of the British Army

In 1914 the British Army contained about 250,000 men. Its two major components, the infantry and the cavalry, were divided into regiments, each with its own history and traditions. Before the war most infantry regiments had two active battalions, each of 1,000 men, plus a part time territorial battalion. Each battalion was divided into four companies and a company consisted of four platoons (usually lettered A-D). There were approximately 50 men in each platoon, under the command of a lieutenant or second lieutenant, with the help of a sergeant. Within each platoon were 4 sections of about 12 men. The cavalry had a similar organisation, but used different terms.

When war broke out the basic structure remained the same but the number of battalions in each regiment grew. For example, at the end of the war there were over 20 York and Lancaster battalions.

By the end of the War over 9 million men and women from the British Isles and the Empire had served in the armed forces.

Volunteering and Conscription

When war broke out there was great enthusiasm amongst young men to enlist. It was widely believed that the war would not last long and so many were keen to join up before the adventure was over. An appeal was made on 7th August 1914 for men of good health between 19 and 30 to enlist. On 12th August it was announced that anyone between the age of 19 and 42 could enlist if they were in good health and at least 5'3" tall. The York and Lancaster and the King's Own Yorkshire Light Infantry were the two most popular regiments amongst Sheffield men.

The Government initially asked for 100,000 men. 750,000 enlisted in the first month and by January 1915 over a million had volunteered. However, from then numbers started to drop and it was quickly realised that huge numbers of men were going to be needed. Conscription was introduced in January 1916, initially for single men aged between 18 and 41. Within a few months married men were also included. The upper age limit was 58 by the end of the war.

Medals

Men and women who served during the war were awarded campaign medals. The most common ones are as follows:

Medals of William Linley

The 1914 Star. This was awarded to those who served in France and Belgium between 5 August 1914 and 22 November 1914.

The 1914/1915 Star. Awarded to those who served in a theatre of war between 5 August 1914 and 31 December 1915.

The British War Medal was awarded to all those who served overseas, though not necessarily in the theatre of war, between 5 August 1914 and 11 November 1918.

The Victory Medal was awarded to all those who served in a theatre of war between 5 August 1914 and 11 November 1918.

Less commonly awarded were the Military Medal and the Military Cross. The Medal was awarded to servicemen who were not officers for 'bravery in battle'. The Cross was awarded to Officers for 'gallantry in the field during active operations'.

Silver Badge

The Silver Badge was awarded to a serviceman who was invalided out of the services. It was found to be necessary as a man of the right age and not in uniform was likely to be challenged as he went about his daily business. The Silver Badge showed that a man had served his country and suffered injury or illness as a result.

Pensions and War Gratuity

Of the few records that exist, many are pension records. From these we can see how carefully a pension was calculated, based on the number of days a man had spent on active service with leave and punishment days excluded. The dependents of every serviceman who died as a result of active service were awarded a pension. Similarly serving personnel who were incapacitated were eligible. When figures are given for a pension award, it is a weekly amount.

The War Gratuity was introduced in 1918 and was payable to any man or his dependents who had served at home for more than 6 months and for any period overseas. The calculation depended on a man's rank and his length of service.

The Chain of Evacuation

A man's chances of survival depended very much on how quickly he could be treated after he had sustained an injury. The Royal Army Medical Corps was not a fighting force. Its members were unarmed and yet went into the most dangerous situations to retrieve injured servicemen. A system was

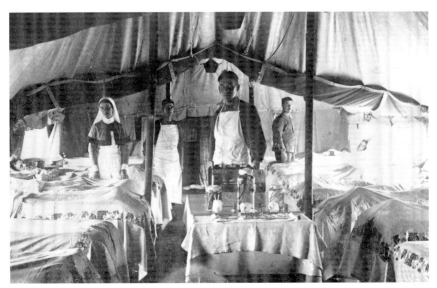

Casualty clearing station

13

established which was called the Chain of Evacuation which efficiently removed men from the front line and ensured that they received the most appropriate treatment.

The first station was the Regimental Aid Post which was as near to the fighting as possible. Here a wounded man received first aid. From here he was taken to the Advanced Dressing Station where further treatment could be given. There could be a Main Dressing Station further back from the front line and from here a seriously injured man would be taken to a Field Ambulance. The Field Ambulance was a mobile medical unit with medical staff and proper treatment areas. From here, if necessary, a man would go to the Casualty Clearing Station, which was a much larger unit with perhaps 50 beds and room for 150 stretchers. These were usually situated up to 20 km behind the front line. A man could stay here for up to 4 weeks. From here a man could recover and re-join his unit, or, if necessary, be transported by ambulance train to near to the coast.

The Base areas such as Etaples, Rouen and Boulogne, Le Havre and Le Touquet had large, fully equipped hospitals. These were Stationary and General hospitals - Stationary hospitals could hold 400 casualties each and the General Hospital over 1000. If a man needed further treatment he would be transferred home from here, usually on a hospital ship.

Sheffield hospitals

The flow of casualties threatened to overwhelm existing facilities and general military hospitals were established all over the country. Sheffield's was called the Third Northern General Hospital. This was the Base hospital, and was situated at the junction of Collegiate Crescent and Ecclesall Road, now part of Sheffield Hallam University. There were also 50 or so associated units in school buildings, private homes and even the Bramall Lane Cricket Pavilion. In addition, the Wadsley Asylum became the Wharncliffe War hospital. Sheffield was able to provide more than 6,000 beds for military patients. When they reached the convalescent stage these men could be seen in the streets of Sheffield wearing their regulation light blue uniforms.

Base hospital,
Ecclesall Road,
Sheffield

War memorial in Sheffield General Cemetery

Servicemen buried in the General Cemetery

While injuries from shellfire were the most common cause of death, soldiers were also killed and injured by sniper fire, grenades and in face to face skirmishes. Officers in particular were always targeted by snipers. Servicemen also died because of faulty weaponry or ammunition, accidents during training, gas poisoning, dysentery, tuberculosis and influenza. Abdominal injuries frequently led to death because of infection. The men buried in the General Cemetery had reached home only to die of their injuries or from illness contracted as a result of active service, sometimes months after they had been discharged from the army.

The men are listed in this chapter in date order according to each one's date of death.

Peter Hibberd

Peter was born in Sheffield in 1883. His mother Katherine, was a widow by 1901 with six children to support. Peter married in 1910 and he and his wife were boarders with a grocer, Thomas Goffin, in Bailey Street. His mother worked as a charwoman and she and three of the other children boarded nearby.

Peter was one of the first to enlist when war broke out. He joined up on 17th August 1914 and became a private in the 3rd Battalion of the East Yorkshire Regiment.

He didn't serve abroad and was probably still training when he became ill. He died in hospital in Hull on 15th November 1914 of a thoracic aneurism and empyema – infected tissue in the body cavity. Because his service had been less than six months his wife Lily did not qualify for the war gratuity.

Harold Steeples

Harold was born in Sheffield in 1890 and his father, Harry, was a pen and pocket bladesmith. The family lived on Radford Street and later Bailey Street. By 1911 Harold was not living with the family but we cannot trace him. His parents had had 9 children by this time, four of whom had died.

Harold served with the 3rd Battalion of the King's Own Yorkshire Light Infantry and served in France. He was awarded the 1915 Star, the British and the War Medal. He died in hospital in Hull on 11th April 1916. He left all his estate to Miss Lizzie Milnes. He is buried in a public grave with no Memorial Inscription.

Joseph Wainwright

Joseph Oscar Wainwright was born in 1885. His parents were Henry and Mary; Henry was a silver spoon and fork burnisher. In the 1901 census, Joseph is described as a furniture maker and in 1911 he was a labourer in a

Doctor dressing a wound

Bessemer shop. He was married to Mary Katherine, and they had a child, Arthur. The family lived on Aberdeen Street.

Joseph enlisted with the Royal Army Medical Corps (RAMC) in August 1914. The RAMC was not a fighting force but was responsible for the evacuation and treatment of sick and wounded men. They were not armed and often had to go into very dangerous situations to recover injured soldiers. Joseph served with the 14th and the 17th Field Ambulances. (A Field Ambulance was not a vehicle but a mobile, front-line medical unit.)

There are no service records in existence for Joseph but there is a hospital record that shows that he was treated twice for haemorrhoids during 1915. The next information we have is that of his death in the 1st London General Hospital on the 6th May 1916. He died of a shrapnel wound received in action to his right kidney and spinal cord and of a haemorrhage.

At exactly this time the author Vera Brittain was serving as a Voluntary Aid Detachment nurse (VAD) in this hospital. She described the surgical ward in a letter to her fiancé:

> The nurses hardly occupy the silent-footed gliding role which they always do in story-books and on the state. For one thing there is too much work to be done in a great hurry. For another, the mixture of gramophones and people shouting or groaning after an operation relieves you of the necessity of being quiet as to your footsteps, for it drowns everything else.

Joseph was buried in the General Cemetery in a grave belonging to George Hayworth, an engineer. We can find no connection between the men.

George Forrest

George was born in Heeley in 1891. He signed up for the Territorial Force in 1908 with the York and Lancs. He was promoted to sergeant in April 1914. When war broke out he was working in a munitions factory but like other men serving in the Territorials he was embodied – called up for active service – on the 5th August 1914.

He was sent abroad with the expeditionary force in April 1915. The records that exist are very difficult to read but we know that he was serving overseas

Case No. 460

1916.

No. 492 Sergeant Forrest G. 1/4th York and Lancs Regt.,
Age 25 years   8½ months.

Nephritis.

March 17th.	Began with pain at the bottom of the back, and also in the stomach 14 days ago.
	Was quite well and working up to this attack.
	Later he noticed his feet and legs started to swell but persisted to work until three days ago.
	Thinks he has not passed sufficent urine.
	Notaced blood in the urine.
	PRESENT CONDITION:-
	Very pale. No oedema in face ;
	Oedema of feet and legs.
	Urine S.Gravity 1010. Alk. Albumen
	Heart. Heart sounds weak. 2nd Aortic and pulmonary
March 20th.	Amount of urine passed during last 24 hours equals 80 oz
	Oedema of legs and feet has disappeared
	℥ Mist. mag. sulph with sod. sulp. morning & nigh
	Diet. Milk Barley water, Lemon water
March 23rd.	Rather more albumen.
April 10th	Fish potatoes, tea and bread and butter. Milk puddings To go on the veranda.
May 7th	Albumen 11%
May 7th	Albumen 7%
May 19th	At Royal Infirmary. Water Test.

6am	75	1019	.01415	1.06
7am	32	1022	.01456	.457
8am	23.5	1018	.00547	1128
9am	30	1008	.00560	.168
10am	32	1008	.00623	.198
11am	17	1018	.00556	.094
	102.5			.5034

June 8th	Spoon diet.
	To Winter Street Hospital

(Signed) N.J.Wigram   T
Capt R.A.M.C.

June 16th	Alb. Blood trace 625 c.c.
June 19th	Cough. Vomiting twice in day.
June 20th	Better Alb increased 750 c.c. T.N.5.5.
June 22nd.	710c.c. T.cl 0.426 2000 Diastase T.N.5.27
	No sickness since 19th.
June 24th	655 c.c. Trace chloride only.
June 28th	Bad night B.O. 5 with blood Urine 235 cc
June 29th	Vomiting B.O. 1. Urine 40 cc Blood in vomit
	Pack causes no sweating
June 30th	Urine 32 cc B.P.80 No sweating.
July 1st	Urine 10 c.c. or less. Vomiting and pain in
	epigastrium the chief complaint.
July 2nd	Died at 5/20am.

The medical records of George Forrest

when he was wounded in the nose and cheek in 1915 and sent back to England to hospital.

At some point he was discharged from the Army and once again engaged in munition work. Sheffield was an important centre for the manufacture of munitions and a Committee on Munitions was established in Sheffield, as in other towns, to trace men serving in the forces who were skilled in munition manufacture. Over 2500 such men were traced and sent back from active service to work in the munitions factory. It is likely that George was one of these.

In March 1916 George became ill and was admitted to hospital. There is a detailed description of his illness, including the food that he ate and the date that he was put on the veranda for fresh air. The last lines of this report make sad reading. He is described on 1st July as suffering 'vomiting and pain'. He died of acute nephritis in the Winter Street Hospital on the 2nd July 1916. His daughter, Mary Kathleen, was born less than a month later.

His wife received a pension and the £15 war gratuity. She was sent George's three medals.

John Philip Chellingworth

John Philip Chellingworth was born in Birmingham in 1898. In 1901 the family address was 'back of 135 Spring Hill, Birmingham'. By 1911 the family, father Frederick John and mother Charlotte Georgina, were in Sheffield, living on Kearsley Road. Frederick was a printer's reader for a newspaper.

John must have been a very gifted artist as he won a scholarship to the Sheffield

Painting of students at Sheffield School of Art

21

School of Art. This would have been quite unusual for a man from a humble background. He enlisted on the 6ᵗʰ October 1915 and joined the Coldstream Guards. He was given the rank of Lance Corporal. We have no military records, just the medal record card which shows that he was awarded the War and the Victory Medals and mistakenly gives him the rank of Private. There is also a record of his effects at the time of his death – his outstanding pay of £7 10s 10d went to his father.

According to the death certificate John died of appendicitis with abscess, peritonitis and heart failure on the 24ᵗʰ November 1916 at the age of 18. The Sheffield Evening Telegraph published a sad obituary on 27ᵗʰ November:

> Art Student Soldier's death
>
> Many friends in Sheffield will hear with keen regret of the death of Lance Corporal John Philip Chellingworth of the Coldstream Guards. He enlisted on October 6ᵗʰ 1915 although still under 18 years of age. But he was a fine vigorous specimen of young manhood being over 6 feet 2 inches tall and broad in proportion and looked older than his years. So keen was he on taking his share of the fighting that he would not wait until he had reached the age limit but insisted on going as soon as he could be accepted.
>
> It is a pathetic and tragic coincidence that he reached the hospital in London after some months at the front on October 6ᵗʰ, a year to the day after joining the army. The body is to be brought to Sheffield and the funeral will take place at the General Cemetery tomorrow, part of the service being held at St Matthew's Church whence the coffin will be conveyed on a gun carriage, accompanied by a military escort.
>
> Lance Corporal Chellingworth was a scholarship student at the Sheffield School of Art and had done much promising work that seemed to indicate a successful career. His Father, Mr F J Chellingworth, is a member of the staff of the Sheffield Telegraph.

Recently Sheffield Hallam University, when undertaking research prior to mounting an exhibition to mark the centenary of the War, came across a black and white photograph of an unfinished painting by a former art student of the Sheffield School of Art. The painting is of five young men, including the artist William Brearley. The original painting had been lost during the Sheffield Blitz of the Second World War but records showed that it had been given to the School of Art by Gladys Chellingworth. We can safely assume that this was John's younger sister. The information the University has is that three of the five men did not return from the war. It is tempting to imagine that one of the men in the picture is John Philip Chellingworth.

Francis Gautier

Francis was born in 1871 in Wakefield. His father, Pierre Louis, was French - born in Paris and was a traveller for a wine and spirit merchant. His mother, Matilda, was from Sheffield. In 1881 the family were living in Norfolk Lane, Sheffield. Matilda was a widow and a charwoman. Pierre Louis had died in 1879 and is buried in the General Cemetery.

In 1901 Francis had married Edna and was a police constable, living in Broad Oaks, Attercliffe with their three-year-old son, Albert. By 1911 the family were in Broomhall Street and had four sons, Albert, Herbert, Wilfred and Pierre Louis. A daughter, Edna Marie, known as Marie, was born in the spring of 1911. Francis was still working as a police constable.

Francis enlisted with the 11th Battalion of the Cheshire Regiment in 1914 and was made a sergeant. He was serving in France in September 1915. He became ill and in April 1916 he wrote a touching letter of farewell to his young daughter. He was transferred to Sheffield and died of stomach cancer on 11 June 1916 in the Royal Infirmary.

PC F H Gautier

His son Albert, mentioned later in this book, was killed in action in August

23

1915. The Gautier family had other losses, including Wilfred who died in 1921, as a result of an accident, at the age of 16 whilst serving with the West Yorkshire Regiment.

Thomas Whiting (Thomas Little)

Thomas was born in 1879 to Tom and Mary Little. His father was an engineer's tool planer. Thomas's father died and his mother re-married in 1884. She married John Henry Whiting who had two sons. Mary had three children, Thomas, Alfred and Polly and in 1891 the family were living in Hermitage Street. John Whiting was a boiler riveter and Mary was a fishing net maker. Ten years later Mary and John had had four children together and Thomas had joined the King's Own Yorkshire Light Infantry (KOYLI) and adopted his stepfather's name. He was living in barracks in Pontefract.

By the time war broke out Thomas had left the KOYLI but was in the Reserve. He enlisted immediately. He was 5' 8" tall and had a 38" chest. In November of 1914 he was sent to France but in January 1915, at Arras, he was wounded and sent back to England. One of the medical reports details his condition. The doctor writes:

> He received a bullet wound in the right forearm when in the trenches and was sent to Base Hospital in Leeds. The wound healed but he has lost power and grip with his right hand… when in furlough [*on leave*] after leaving Leeds hospital he developed an attack of acute nephritis and was treated for this in hospital at Sheffield from 20th April 1915 to 12th May 1915.

Regarding his present medical condition, the doctor continues:

> There is thickening of the bone and slight deformity of the right ulna. There is odema of both legs and urine contains albumen.

The report of the medical board concludes that although the injury to his arm was likely to recover, there was evidence of Bright's disease - kidney disease - which would 'tend to get worse'. He was discharged as permanently unfit on the 19th June 1915. He died on the 28th November 1916 of nephritis.

John Lindop

John was born in 1886 to Albert and Sarah. He married Florence - Florrie - Swindel in April 1909. They had three children, Albert, Reginald and Florence. Florrie was six months pregnant with Albert when they got married at St Silas Parish Church.

When he enlisted with the York and Lancs on 11 December 1915, John was 29 years old. He was a van salesman. He was 5'4" tall and had a chest measurement of 34 ½".

Just over a year later John died of meningitis in Clipstone Court hospital. He was stationed at Clipstone Camp, Mansfield. (This was one of the largest training camps in the country. It could hold upwards of 30,000 men at a time when the population of Mansfield was about 37,000.)

The following year Florrie was given a pension of 26s 3d a week for herself and her three children. The pension records show that the disease was contracted during military service.

Florrie remarried at the end of 1918 to Charles Wells but she ensured that John's medals were sent to her at her new address.

Clipstone Camp

Tom Mosely

Tom was born in 1890 to Tom and Maggie Mosely. His father was a saw maker. Tom married Jessie Beaumont in the spring of 1908. Their first son, Thomas Lewis, was born later that year and they had a second baby, Frank, born in 1912. Tom was a hairdresser.

Records show that Tom signed up for the duration of the War on 11 December 1915. He gave his occupation as hairdresser but also described himself as a motor engineer and that his preferred corps would be motor transport. The medical examination shows that he was 5'6" tall and weighted 140lbs. He was appointed to the Army Service Corps as a Motor Transport Learner.

Sadly, the next information we have is of Tom's death. He died in Hounslow Barrack hospital of bronchitis on 20 January 1917. We have the final medical report which details his last days. Parts of it are illegible but it makes thought-provoking reading a hundred years later:

14.1.17 Acute broncho-pneumonia. Cardiac dilatation [*enlarged heart*]. Admitted respiration 32 pulse 120 temp …. *illegible*. Marked dyspnoea [*shortness of breath*] … patches of broncho-pneumonic consolidation in lower lobes of both lungs

15.1.17 Very little sleep. Dyspnoea still marked. No lividity [*discolouration*]. Lung condition much the same.

16.1.17 Mixture containing strychnine and digitalis given. Poultice to chest and brandy two-hourly.

17.1.17 No improvement. Restless and getting no sleep. Extension of consolidated area in both lungs and behind. Some slight lividity. Strychnine hypodermically. Antiphlogistine poultice.

18.1.17 Getting worse. Heart sounds rapid and feeble, marked restlessness and delirium.

19.1.17 Temperature still continuous 101 deg – 103 deg. Pulse 130 compressible. Respiration 40-50. Lividity marked

20.1.17 Died 11.15pm

Jessie was awarded a weekly pension of 22s 11d for herself and her two children.

Clifton Braithwaite

Clifton was born in 1889 to William and Annie. His father was a silversmith. By 1911 Clifton was married to Ada Walker and they had had a child who had died. The couple were married in the first quarter of 1911 and the Census was taken in April 1911 so it seems likely that Ada was pregnant when they got married. Clifton was a tailor's assistant.

He joined the Army Service Corps (ASC). This is the corps of the army that is responsible for transport and supply and its members are often considered to be unsung heroes. Its nickname, Ally Sloper's Cavalry (named after a cartoon character known for laziness and sloping off), belies the fact that the tremendous organisation behind the logistical nightmare of supplying the troops was one of the reasons the war was won. After the War the ASC was awarded the 'Royal' prefix in recognition of its service.

Army Service Corps recruitment poster

We have no military records for Clifton so we do not know where he served. He was taken ill and sent to the Davidson War Hospital in Croydon. There he died on 9th March 1917 of chronic bronchitis and emphysema, leaving behind his young widow and a child. She was not entitled to a war gratuity and received only £1 19s and 7d.

Albert Charles Stevens

Albert was born in Gibraltar to Henry and Harriett Stevens in 1862. Henry was a career soldier in the Royal Engineers. Albert went to the School of

Military Engineering in Chatham, Kent. This was a school where boys were taught sapping – digging trenches or undermining fortifications, mining and other military fieldwork. Boys who couldn't read and write were taught to do so, and those that could read were taught to read plans. The school, now the Royal School of Military Engineering continues to train Royal Engineers, the lowest rank of whom is known as a Sapper.

Albert Stevens

Albert married Isabella Epworth in 1886 and continued his career as a soldier. Isabella was from Sheffield and her brothers were cutlers. Albert and Isabella's first daughter, Mary Isabella was born in Edinburgh where Albert was serving as a Sergeant Major. Lillian Rose was born in Sheffield and Grace Eileen was born in County Westmeath, Ireland.

In 1917 Albert died in the 3rd Northern General Hospital. He left his estate of over £900 to Isabella's brothers, Thomas and Joseph Epworth, not his wife. By 1922 Isabella and her three daughters had emigrated to Canada. On the journey out there she met James Wilson, a man nine years her junior, whom she married less than a year later. However, the marriage didn't work out and she returned to Sheffield alone. When she died in 1940 she was buried with her first husband in the Cemetery.

The Memorial Inscription reads:

In loving memory of Albert Charles Stevens, late Captain R E, dearly beloved husband of Isabella Stevens, died May 21 1917 aged 55 years. At rest.

William Linley

The Commonwealth War Graves Commission was established in 1917 to record the details of every man or woman who died as a result of armed conflict. The task was huge, so it is inevitable that there are occasionally omissions. We believe that one such is William Linley. He is not recorded on the CWGC website and was not accorded a CWGC gravestone in the Cemetery as other men were.

William Linley was born in 1883 and his grandfather was a scythemaker from Norton, then in Derbyshire. His father Samuel was a cab driver who died at the age of 43. His mother, Mary, was born in Ireland and, as was so common, she raised the family by herself. The family lived in Angus Square.

We have little information about William until he enlisted 21 August 1914, at the very beginning of the war. His occupation was groom, and it was probably for this reason he joined the Army Service Corps where he became a driver. Transport was moving away from mainly horse-drawn to mechanised vehicles and many men quickly learnt new skills to ensure future employment. He was 5'4" tall, with a chest size of 36" and he weighed 9 ½ stone.

William's pension records show that he was in France from the 6th November 1914 until the 24th March 1917. He became ill in France in January 1917. He had swellings in the right side of his head and neck which were diagnosed as tuberculous. As was normal for medical reports it was considered important to establish whether the illness was due to active service or as a result of personal neglect. The medics concluded that the illness and consequent disability was due to 'exposure to weather and hardship of active military service'. William was sent back to England in March 1917, to Tooting Grove hospital. He had six operations from April to August to clean out the glands but these were unsuccessful. Eventually further operations were 'not advised' and William was discharged as 100% medically unfit on 7th November 1917. He was sent to the Royal Infirmary, Sheffield where he died on 5th January 1918. His brother Percy was with him. His War Gratuity was paid to his brother Samuel.

Samuel applied for William's medals in 1927 and they then passed to his daughter, Annie.

Wilfred Downes Pollard

Wilfred was born in Eccles, Lancashire in 1884 where his father, William, was an architect. Downes was his mother's maiden name and all the boys in the family had this as a middle name. Wilfred had a twin sister, Ethel. He started work as a bank clerk. The family lived on Bristol Road, Brocco Bank, Sheffield.

Wilfred enlisted with the 12th Battalion of the York and Lancaster Regiment. We have no military records for him but there is a hospital record which shows that he had a gunshot wound of his left leg on the 4th July 1916 and was sent home on the hospital ship, Panama. At this time the Regiment was heavily involved in the Battle at Serre on the Somme. Wilfred returned to France and transferred to the Notts and Derby Regiment of the Sherwood Foresters where he received a commission in October 1917.

York and Lancs Chapel in Sheffield Cathedral

He died in Southmead Hospital, Bristol of a gunshot wound to his right foot and pneumonia on 26 April 1918. The National Probate Calendar shows that he left over £600 to his father. His twin sister had died in 1914.

Fred Harrison

Fred was born in 1882 to Mary and Joseph, who lived on Prince Street, Sheffield. Joseph was a file forger. Fred became a silversmith and married Mary Ellen.

Fred enlisted in 1916. As he was a silversmith it must have seemed a natural progression to become a coppersmith in the Royal Naval Air Service, which later became the Royal Air Force (RAF). He would be employed repairing aeroplanes. His Air Force pay was 4 shillings a week and he enlisted for the duration of the war.

His military records do not exist but we know that he was with the 28th Squadron which was a training squadron. He became ill with pneumonia and died on the 10th July 1918 in the Military Hospital in Chiseldon, Wiltshire. According to the death certificate, his wife was present at the death.

William James and Frank Osguthorpe

Wilfred Osguthorpe, the father of the two soldiers who died, was born in 1857 in Sheffield and served with the South Yorkshire Regiment. He married Sarah Croucher in Hampshire in September 1889 and she travelled with him as he was posted around the country. As a result, their children were born in the Channel Islands, in Ireland and in Sheffield. Wilfred served with the Yorkshire Light Infantry and was in South Africa during 1899-1902.

The family had a daughter, Lily May and three sons, Wilfred Maurice, William James and Frank. All three sons enlisted. William James was born in Belfast. In 1911 he was a spiral spring maker. He joined the Yorkshire Light Infantry and was later transferred to the Labour Corps. In April 1917 a number of infantry battalions were transferred to the Labour Corps and William served with one of these. He first served in Western Europe in August 1915 and he was discharged from the army in May 1918. The nature

Mrs Osguthorpe and her sons

of his disability was given as 'debility'. A living relative believes that William was gassed and this resulted in ill health. He died on 20th August 1920 of tuberculosis of the lungs and cardiac failure.

The records of Springfield Board School on Cavendish Street show that Frank was a pupil there until just before his 14th birthday when he left to become a razor grinder. Frank joined the Army for the duration of the war in April 1917. He transferred to the Royal Flying Corps (RFC) in February 1918. This came into being in March 1912 as a result of an Act of Parliament. Frank became a fitter, responsible for repairing aircraft.

The two wings of the RFC, the naval and the military, were unified and the Royal Air Force (RAF) came into being on the 1 April 1918. Frank immediately became part of this new organisation. He was based at RAF Bekesbourne in Kent. On the 21st August 1918 Frank was accidentally killed whilst swinging the propeller of an aeroplane.

The Sheffield Evening Telegraph of 29th August 1918 carried this obituary:

Osguthorpe. At Bekesbourne, Canterbury. After accident August 25th. Air mechanic Frank Osguthorpe aged 19 ½. Dearly beloved youngest son of Mrs W Osguthorpe of 22 Stalker Lees Road, Sheffield and dearly loved brother of Mrs S Williamson, 23 Havelock Square. Interment General Cemetery Friday 2 o'clock with full military honours. Deeply mourned.

The eldest brother, Wilfred, survived the war and moved to Brighton where he ran a guest house for many years. His grandson recalls that Wilfred was gassed during the war and he claimed he survived because he was much shorter than his brothers who made better targets.

Arthur Thomas Lea

Arthur was born in 1884 to Cornelius and Margaret. Cornelius was a cabinet case maker - he made cutlery cases - and the family lived on Cavendish Street. By 1901 Arthur was working with his father and brother and the family were able to employ a servant. In 1908 Arthur married Alice Doglas Lea and the couple lived next door to his parents. According to the 1911 census they had had a baby but it had died. By this time Cornelius had started the Sheffield Cardboard Box company and Arthur continued to work for his father.

However, by the time he enlisted in 1916 Arthur was a Post Office telephonist and for this reason wanted to join the Royal Engineers as a signaller. His wife's mother, Jane Hendry, was a postmistress and stationer on Glossop Road and it is possible that Arthur worked for her. He wasn't called up until 1917 when he was given a medical and was considered to be class B1 – a medical category which assessed Arthur as free from serious organic diseases and able to march 5 miles. He was approved as a Royal Engineers Telephonist and sent to Fenny Stratford signal department for training. He was 33 years old, 5' 7" tall with a 28" chest. His complexion was described as 'sallow'.

After five months' training Arthur was posted to France and served with the 4th Signal Corps. He reported sick on the 2nd June 1918 and we have a medical report:

The patient lived in a damp cellar for 3 months where he developed a cough, loss of energy and slight haemoptysis *[coughing up blood]* … he was admitted with great pain in his pharynx and a bad cough… there is slight moisture in both lungs. Evidence of the disease TB is present in sputum. Patient rather emaciated.

The Officer in medical charge of the case stated that the illness and resultant disability was 'attributable to service during the present war'. Arthur was considered to be suffering 100% disability and was discharged as permanently unfit to a sanatorium.

Arthur was evacuated back to Sheffield and on the 10th September 1918 in Crimicar Lane hospital he died of tuberculosis of the lungs and larynx.

Royal Engineer telephonist in the field

Allan Armstrong

Allan Armstrong was born in 1897 to Lewis and Kate Armstrong in Huddersfield. Lewis was a general labourer and by 1901 the family were living in Porter Street, Sheffield.

Allan enlisted in Sheffield on 2 December 1915 at the age of 18. He became a Private in the 9th Battalion of the Glasgow Highlanders in the Highland Light Infantry.

Unusually some of Allan's records have survived so we know that when he joined up he was a copy reader in a newspaper office. There is also a physical description of Allan, written when he was examined in May 1916. The description says that he was 5' 2½" tall and weighed 95lbs. This would make him 6 ½ stone which seems very small indeed. Allan had a scar above his right eye and vaccination marks. He was declared 'fit for service at home' but described as having 'slight defects but not enough to cause rejection'. There is a handwritten note on his records which says that he would 'improve with training'. He began his training on the 12th May 1916 and just over a year later he was sent to France.

Allan arrived in France on 2 June 1917 and was wounded in the field on September 26th 1917. He received a shrapnel wound to the ilium – the pelvic bone. By October 8th 1917 he was in the 1st Southern General Hospital which was in Birmingham, having travelled via Boulogne and Antwerp. It appears that the wound became septic and the infection spread to the abdominal cavity and he endured several 'scraping' operations. In February 1918 an x-ray showed a foreign body in the lumbar region which was removed. He was discharged on 2 July 1918. The report states that the wounds had healed but that Allan had a great deal of pain. The Army Medical Board was of the opinion that he was suffering total disability but that this would reduce. His military character was described as 'very good' and a 'sober, honest and diligent soldier, discharged in consequence of a wound sustained in action'. He was entitled to wear one strip of gold braid – also known as the wound stripe.

He died on 28 September 1918 at 74 Cemetery Road, Doncaster. The death certificate records that he died of 'valvular disease of the heart and syncope'. He was 21 years old.

He is remembered on the Sheffield Telegraph and Sheffield Council Roll of Honour.

Serial Number ℋ63 ℋ.1.

"Wanting Records" etc...

R.A.S.N 5910

Army Form B. 268.

This space to be left blank for the Chelsea Number.

Proceedings on Discharge.

(When forwarded for confirmation the documents named on page 4 should be enclosed.)

No. 241731.　　Army Rank　Private

Name　Allan Armstrong
(The name must agree strictly with that on enlistment, unless changed subsequently by authority.)

Corps　**HIGHLAND LIGHT INFANTRY**

Battalion, Battery, Company, Depôt, &c.　9 Bn (Depot)
(If attached to the Regular Establishment of the Special Reserve, or Permanent Staff of the Territorial Force, &c., or to General Staff of the Army, it should be so stated.)

Date of discharge　2 July 18

Place of discharge　Birmingham

1.　　　Description at the time of discharge.

Age　20　years　5　months　　Descriptive marks.
Height　5　feet　3　inches　Scar 5" long Right thigh
Chest measurement { girth when fully expanded　32½　ins.
{ range of expansion　2½　ins.
Complexion
Eyes　Brown
Hair　Brown
Trade　Copy Reader
Intended place of residence　71 Ashford Road Sharrow Sheffield
(To be given as fully as practicable)

(The measurements and description should be carefully taken on the day the man leaves his unit, but in the case of men sent home from abroad for discharge, the age and intended place of residence should be left blank to be filled in by the Officer who confirms the discharge at home.)

2.　The above-named man is discharged in consequence of　being NO LONGER PHYSICALLY FIT FOR WAR SERVICE

Kings Regulations Para 392 XVI

(The cause of discharge must be worded as prescribed in the King's Regulations and be identical with that on the discharge certificate. If discharged by superior authority, the No. and date of the letter to be quoted.)

3.　Military character :—　V good.

4.　Character awarded in accordance with King's Regulations :—
A sober, honest, & diligent soldier — discharged in consequence of a wound sustained in action

Entitled to wear the stripe of Gold Braid

Certified that the above is an accurate copy of the character given by me on Army B. 2067* and that Army Form B. 2089 was awarded in this case.

　　　　　　　　Col.
Initials of Commanding Records,
No 2 District.

Army Form B. 2088 has been issued to*

D. D. & L., London, E.C.
(A5689) WL W7772/M2846 500,000 8/17 Sch. 32　Forms B. 268　41

* Strike out if not applicable.

[OVER.

Medical records for Allan Armstrong

William Spencer Yates

William was born in 1900, to William and Ada Yates. William senior was a silversmith and by 1911 the family were living in South View Crescent. William had five siblings and he worked for a butcher on Saturdays but was at school for the rest of the week.

He joined the Royal Naval Volunteer Reserve, Division Tyne, on the 16 May 1918, three months before his 18th birthday. He was 5' 6" tall, with fair hair, dark grey eyes, a fresh complexion and a chest of nearly 32". William then was sent to Crystal Palace, London which was used as a training establishment during the war and was known as HMS Victory VI. He began his training there in July 1918. His character was described as very good and his ability was satisfactory. Unfortunately, he was soon taken ill and he died of double pneumonia on the 8th October 1918. Four days later, his little brother Jack, aged 6, also died.

Charles Littlehales

Charles was born in 1894 and the family lived in Moore Street, Broomhall, Sheffield. His father, Samuel, was an electro plate silver finisher. He had an older brother who was a miner, and in 1911 Charles was a bricklayer's labourer.

Charles joined the 4th (Hallamshire) Battalion of the York and Lancaster Regiment as a territorial soldier in February 1910. At this time, he was 17 years old and a German silver caster. He signed on for four years. He was 5'3" tall and weighed 119 lbs. He had grey eyes and brown hair. He attended a preliminary training but was discharged after 72 days to join the Special Reserve of the York and Lancs. There is a note on his record from Sergeant R. Angel who visited the clerk of the company for which Charles worked asking for a character reference: 'Mr Hancock knows nothing wrong of the lad, only that he is enlisting against his parents' wish.' Charles attended training and was promoted to Lance Corporal but lost this rank when he went absent for 6 days.

Charles married Emma Hopewell in April 1913 and as a Reservist was one of the first to be called up on the 4th August 1914. A few days later his son was born. Charles was posted on the 9th December 1914 to France.

Charles Littlehales' enlistment form

On 8th August 1915, at Hooge, Charles was wounded and crushed in a trench. This was one of the bloodiest battles at Ypres. The village of Hooge was lost and won several times and at the end of the war it was completely destroyed. Charles was treated in France and in January 1916 was appointed an unpaid Lance Corporal. In May of 1916 he was in hospital again with 'Pyrexia of Unknown Origin' – what we know now as trench fever. Charles recovered but received a gun shot wound to the shoulder and thigh in September 1916. He was sent back to England for treatment but was back in France on the 3rd March 1917.

In April 1917 Charles is allowed to go back to England to resume working for William Turner's who are now a controlled firm engaged in munitions work. The terms of engagement during the war were different for those who had signed up with the Reserves before the war. When their term finished, they were allowed to leave, although efforts would be made to persuade them to stay and they could be conscripted. Because he went to work in munitions, Charles was able to return to his family.

Map of Hooge

In July 1917 Charles is formally discharged and he writes to the administrators of the York and Lancs regiment to ask for his silver war badge.

Unfortunately, Charles became ill and on the 2nd November 1918 he died of influenza and pneumonia. Attached to his military records is a letter from Dr W O Arnold of 96 Hanover St, Sheffield who says that the man 'was under my care for some time previous, suffering from weakness of lungs, due to being buried on active service. This, I am of the opinion, tended to hasten his death'.

Emma had two small children and remarried. She received Charles' medals in 1922.

Albert Henry Rodgers

Albert was born in 1890 to Alfred Hartley Rodgers and his wife Emily. Alfred was a razor strop maker and the family lived in Eldon Street. Emily died in 1894 leaving Alfred with five children. He quickly married again, to Hannah Ellin and they had another child.

At the age of 18, in 1908, Albert joined the Army. He joined the 6th Dragoons, choosing this regiment as a friend had already enlisted. He gave his occupation as 'draftsman'. Part of his attestation form exists and it shows that he was considered 'a very good class of recruit'. He was nearly 5'7", weighed 114lbs and had a chest measurement of 35". There is reference from Mr Micklethwaite, a grocer, who had known him for 10 years which says that he is 'sober and honest'. He signed on for 12 years, intending to spend 7 years in the regular army and 5 in the reserve.

Albert was transferred to the 3rd Prince of Wales Dragoon Guards and served in Abyssinia and Egypt – he had a spell in hospital with tonsillitis in Cairo. His employment sheet states that he is an 'honest, sober and well educated man. Clean, reliable and trustworthy. Intelligent. A good clerk and signaller'. He was promoted to Corporal in 1913.

By October 1914 he was serving in France. In April 1915 and again in June

Canadian hospital war diary

40

1915 he was mentioned in despatches for 'gallant and distinguished service in the field'. He was promoted to sergeant. In November 1916 Albert received a permanent commission with the Royal Field Artillery. He was made a Lieutenant with the 4th (Reserve) Brigade.

Sadly, the next information we have about Albert is news of his death. The War Diary for the No. 15 Canadian Red Cross Hospital in Taplow, Bucks, records his death on the 7th November 1918, four days before the Armistice was signed. He died of influenza and bronchopneumonia. He left nearly £300 to his brother, Alfred Rodgers of Hunter House Road, Sheffield.

William Frederick Ashton

William Frederick, known always as Frederick, was born in 1885 to William and Lucy in the village of Shebbear, Devon. In 1891 William was a poulterer and fishmonger and the family lived on Erbington Street in Plymouth – a street still lined with independent shops. By 1901, Frederick was an assistant to his father in the shop but by 1911 he was a United Methodist Minister in Stockton on Tees.

Frederick began his training as a Minister in the Woodbrooke Settlement in Birmingham. Woodbrooke was founded in 1903 as a Quaker Study Centre. Local Quaker and chocolate maker George Cadbury donated his former home for the purpose. Frederick studied there in the

Woodbrooke Settlement

Spring and Summer terms of 1908. He also studied at the United Methodist College, Manchester – the college was renamed in 1906 after industrialist Sir William Hartley.

Frederick was ordained as a Minister in the United Methodist Church in 1910. He initially worked in Stockton on Tees, near Sunderland. There he was examined as a probationer in 1913 and it was reported in a local newspaper that 'the District Committee who examined him gave an excellent report'. He then came to Sheffield and was a Minister at the

Tinsley Methodist Chapel. There is mention of him conducting a marriage in a newspaper of 1917. The chapel no longer exists. It was demolished in 1964 and replaced with a new building in 1981.

On the 8th July 1918 Frederick became a temporary Chaplain with the West Riding Regiment (Volunteer Forces). By the 28th August he was with the West Yorkshire Regiment, still as a temporary Chaplain and on the 5th November he was appointed an Honorary Chaplain to the Forces. He was attached to the Northern Aircraft Repair Depot - a unit of the RAF based at Coal Aston. The RAF had not yet its own chaplains' branch. According to the Museum of Army Chaplaincy, Frederick was the only recorded World War One Chaplaincy casualty serving with the RAF.

Just as the War finished, Frederick contracted pneumonia and was admitted to the Base Hospital on Collegiate Crescent. He died on the 18th of November of pneumonia and heart failure. He left his estate of £285 10s 10d to his brother Henry, a greengrocer in Plymouth.

Joseph William Stanley Pickering

Joseph was born in 1898 to Joseph and Agnes. His father was a provision dealer and the family lived at Alderson Place. Joseph senior spent time in Wakefield Prison for being in arrears with his wife's maintenance. He died in 1904 and by the time of the 1911 census Agnes was a butcheress and living in Gloucester Street. She re-married in 1914.

Joseph joined the Royal Army Medical Corps and served with the 2nd/3rd West Riding Field Ambulance. At the time of his death he was a Private in the 36th Field Ambulance which was serving in France. He died in

Field Ambulance

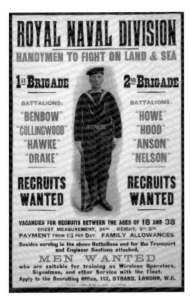

ROYAL NAVAL DIVISION

HANDYMEN TO FIGHT ON LAND & SEA

1ˢᵗ BRIGADE   2ⁿᵈ BRIGADE

BATTALIONS: BATTALIONS:
"BENBOW"   "HOWE"
"COLLINGWOOD"   "HOOD"
"HAWKE"   "ANSON"
"DRAKE"   "NELSON"

RECRUITS WANTED   RECRUITS WANTED

VACANCIES FOR RECRUITS BETWEEN THE AGES OF 18 AND 38
CHEST MEASUREMENT, 34" HEIGHT, 5'-3".
PAYMENT FROM 1/3 PER DAY. FAMILY ALLOWANCES.
Besides serving in the above Battalions and for the Transport
and Engineer Sections attached,
MEN WANTED
who are suitable for training as Wireless Operators,
Signalmen, and other Service with the Fleet.
Apply to the Recruiting Office, 112, STRAND, LONDON, W.C.

Royal Naval Volunteer
Reserve recruitment poster

the Temporary Military Hospital on Collegiate Crescent, Sheffield on 20 November 1918. The cause of death was 'phagodena lip and face (11 days) and septicomia'. Phagodena is a term for serious, deep, necrotic gangrenous skin ulcers which could be caused by bacterial infection or trauma. He was 20 years old. His mother was with him when he died.

Arthur Thompson

Arthur was born in 1898 and by the time of the 1911 census his parents, George, a surgical instrument grinder, and Emma had had 11 children and lost three of them. The family were living on Harwood Street and Arthur was an errand boy.

Arthur enlisted with the Royal Naval Volunteer Reserve (RNVR) as a signalman. The Royal Naval Reserve was originally a reserve of professional seamen from the merchant service and the fishing fleets. In 1903 the RNVR was formed which took a reserve of civilian volunteers. (Many men of the RNVR found themselves serving as infantry when Winston Churchill, as First Lord of the Admiralty, found himself with surplus volunteer sailors and no ships on which they could serve.) The RNVR was divided into divisions whose names were taken from the place where the main centre was based. Men who enlisted for the duration of the War were given the 'Z' prefix to their number, thus Arthur's number began TZ – 'T' for Tyneside.

According to his Service Records when Arthur enlisted he was a machine file cutter, 5' 5" tall with brown hair, dark grey eyes and a 30" chest. He also

HMS Vulcan

lied about his age, saying that he was 19 when in fact he was 17. The record card also states that he couldn't swim. He was drafted to Signal School and then to HMS Vulcan, a training ship based in Scotland. On the 23rd February 1917 he was invalided out of the Navy with pulmonary tuberculosis. He died on December 7th 1918 at the age of 20. He was the fourth of George and Emma Thompson's children to die.

Charles Cheetham

Charles was born in 1867 to William and Mary Cheetham. Charles' father was from London and was a surgical instrument grinder. On 12th August 1878, at the age of 11, Charles was admitted to the Calder Farm Reformatory School in Mirfield. His admission record, which includes a photograph, described four previous crimes, one of stealing and the other three the crime of 'sleeping out' for which he was punished on one occasion with '12 strokes with birch rod'. He was sent to the School for stealing the cap of another boy. On this occasion he was sentenced to 42 days in the House of Correction and 5 years at the Reformatory School. The admission form reports that he had no education and that he had been in the habit of sleeping out for the past four months. There is a physical description too: 11-year-old, Charles was 4 ft 3 ½ inches tall, had a slight figure, pale complexion, brown hair and grey eyes.

Calder Farm Reformatory School was opened in 1855 and took over 100 boys from all over the country. The boys were taught skills such as farming and tailoring

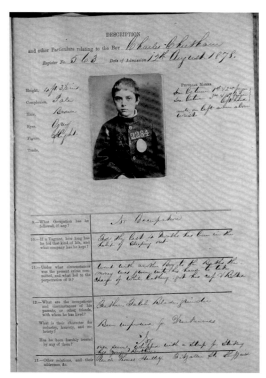

Charles Cheetham's Reform School record

44

(Charles is described as a tailor and scholar in the 1881 Census) as well as being given a conventional education.

In July 1883 Charles was in trouble again. He served 7 days' hard labour in Wakefield Prison for being 'a rogue and a vagabond'. He was committed for the same offence in September of that year. In May the following year Charles served another sentence in prison, with Joshua Johnson, for stealing 2 coats and 8 bottles of stout. They got 3 months' hard labour. In October of the same year the two men were back in prison for stealing a pair of trousers. This time they got 6 months' hard labour.

At the age of 18, a year later, Charles enlisted for 12 years with the West Riding Regiment. He signed on in Halifax and stated that he had never been sentenced to penal servitude or convicted by a civil power. Perhaps this is the reason he travelled to Halifax. His military service sheet is a long list of dates relating to trials, convictions and time spent in prison whilst in the Army. He was eventually discharged in August 1897.

The next evidence for the whereabouts of Charles is that he enlisted to serve in the War on the 3rd December 1914. He served as a driver with the Royal Army Service Corps but changed his name to Charles Foster. This is not unusual - a man with Charles' history would be glad to leave that behind and begin again. His military records are missing but he served throughout the war and was awarded the Star, Victory and British Medals.

Charles Cheetham, who served as Charles Foster, died in Winter Street hospital, Sheffield on 2nd February 1919 of influenza and pneumonia. His sister was with him when he died. Charles is buried in the family grave, but there is no mention of him on the Memorial Inscription.

John Arthur Marriott

John was born in Sheffield in 1894. The family lived in Pearl Street. John's Father, George Ethelbert, was a lamplighter for the Corporation and John and his brothers were cutlers, making pocket knives.

No military records exist for John. All we know is that he served with the 31st Labour Company of the York and Lancaster Regiment. He married Frances Ellen Mabel Hoskings at the beginning of 1919 and on the 7th March of the same year he died in the temporary military hospital on Collegiate Crescent of influenza and pneumonia. Frances remarried - an Ernest Greenhedge in 1922 -and emigrated to Australia.

Walter Andrews Parke

Walter was born Walter Parke in Coltishall, Norfolk in 1874. His father, Charles, was a boat builder, building traditional Norfolk wherries. This trade collapsed in Coltishall with the coming of the railway to the village in 1879, not long after Walter's birth and Charles became a carpenter.

Walter became a soldier. In 1891 he was serving as a private, living in Cavalry barracks in Aldershot. He served in South Africa from March 1900 until July 1901 with the Hussars.

The next information we have is that Walter married Florence Depledge, a Sheffield girl, in 1906. They were both in their mid thirties when they married and they had no children. Florence had been a file cutter, living on Sharrow Vale Road. The couple moved to Wales where Walter, now known as Walter Andrews Parke, became a mason's labourer.

At the age of 40, in October 1914, Walter enlisted with the Welsh (or Welch) Regiment. He enlisted as Walter Andrews and joined the 20th Battalion. His trade was given as haulier, which was a term used at the time for a man who used pit ponies to haul the hewn coal to the surface at a colliery. It is not known why he chose to change his name but this was not uncommon. He was 6' tall and had a chest of 35" and was considered fit for active service.

On the 2nd September 1915 Walter was discharged from the army as no longer fit for active service. His character was considered to be 'very good and his disability was haemorrhoids, for which he had been hospitalised and the medical board considered that 'the man's present condition may be regarded as aggravated by service since the declaration of war'. He was discharged permanently, being 'over age'. Walter's pension records show that his medical condition was reviewed every 6 months and in May 1918 there was a letter from the doctor in Blaengwynfi, Glamorgan, stating that Walter 'was suffering from tuburcle of lung and was incapacitated for work and should receive special treatment as an in-patient in a Sanatorium for an indefinite period'. It was considered that this illness was aggravated by war and that his disability was 100%. A note mentions that the disability caused by his haemorrhoids was only 20%.

Walter died in Wales, on the 20th May 1919, of tuberculosis.

Herbert Stuart

Herbert was born in 1898 in Intake, Sheffield. His father, William John, was a coal miner, working in the Tinsley Park Pit. Herbert followed in his father's footsteps and by the age of 13 he was working at Waverley Pit - a pit adjacent to his father's - 'on belts'. This meant that he would have worked on the surface, picking dirt and stones from the conveyor belt which brought coal out of the pit.

Herbert enlisted in January 1915. His pension records show that at this time he was 19 ½ years old (which he wasn't, he was only 17), was 5' 4" tall and had a 35" chest. His trade was 'washer' – another job at the pit. He would have worked on the machine that washed the coal to remove impurities, ensuring that the machine was kept working and that the water supply was maintained. Later medical reports indicate that Herbert had bronchitis. Men unfit through ill health to work underground were sometimes given work on the surface. Herbert joined the Royal Field Artillery as a driver.

He served in the UK and in France but was discharged in May 1916 as being permanently unfit. He had tuberculosis. The report of the Medical Board describes how Herbert had a history of bronchitis but that the tuberculosis originated at Ypres in the summer of 1915. When he was examined by the medical board he had a cough, haemoptysis – he was spitting blood – and a high fever. It was concluded that his illness was aggravated by active service. He was awarded a Silver War badge, as well as all three medals and a pension.

As was usual practice, this pension was reviewed every 6 months and Herbert's incapacity was getting worse. By December 1917 Albert was considered to be totally incapacitated. He died in Crimicar Lane hospital in June 1919.

Harry Wilson

Harry was born in 1899. His parents were Charles and Henrietta, both born in the North East of England. The family then moved to Nottingham, where Henry and his older brother and sister were born, and finally to Sheffield, where another brother was born. Charles was a timber merchant's clerk. In 1911 the family were living on Penrhyn Road.

All Over Age

The Little Beggars Under Age

You cannot help liking the little chaps who slip the cables from home and join us at the Crystal Palace. Can you condemn a youth who says he *thinks* he is over the minimum age for enrolment ? The most reasonable view to take is one of over-estimation, the result probably of the prevailing hereditary instinctive desire to do one's share of duty.

Medical men gauge the age of people, not by the certificate of birth, but by physical and mental condition. A cultivated man of fifty, accustomed to normal living and outdoor recreation, is a younger man than a drink-sodden navvy of twenty-five. The little recruit of grit and pluck is more of a man at the age of fifteen than the slackers of twenty-one.

It is not possible to keep these young recruits in the Service after discovery of certified under-age ; but we are dead-sure they will leave their parents' apron strings, again and again, until they reach the required age, for they are real chips of that ancient block(-head), John Bull !

The only existing record we have shows that Harry was serving in Western Europe by July 1915. At this time, he would have been barely 16 years old. He served with the King's Own Yorkshire Light Infantry, the Glasgow Highlanders and the Highland Light Infantry.

27

From a Royal Naval Division magazine

He served all through the war and was awarded the 1915 Star as well as the British and Victory medals. He died on 30th July 1919 aged just 20 of pulmonary tuberculosis and syncope.

Thomas Robert Peck

Thomas was born in Sheffield in 1879. He was the son of John and Catherine. John was a general labourer. Ten years later Thomas's mother had died and Thomas and his father were both working in a quarry. In 1904, when he was working as a tramway conductor, Thomas got into debt and served 8 days in Wakefield Prison. Three years later, he married Edna Leak, who was 10 years older than him, and they had two sons, Robert and Albert.

Thomas signed up for the duration of the War in December 1915. He joined the 1/4th Hallamshires York and Lancs Regiment. He was 5'8" tall and weighed 116 lbs. He was described as having 'slight defects' – he had flat feet – but being fit for active service. In December 1916 he was sent to France and for a while was attached to the 185th Tunnelling Company.

On the 18th April, 1918 he reported sick. The officer in charge filled in a form which was marked 'urgent and confidential'.

Thomas R Peck

This report was to be 'rendered in the case of officers and other ranks who, without any visible wound, became non-effective from physical conditions claimed or presumed to have originated from effects of British or enemy weapons in action' - in other words, if a man was suffering from shell shock. The report states that Thomas was transferred through the North Midland Field Ambulance and that he was 'exhausted. Shaken up,' and had a 'septic middle finger of the left hand'. An injury to the left hand was considered to be suspicious as it could be self-inflicted. The soldier stated that the condition was caused by a shell exploding near him at Messines. His Captain, however, stated that Walter was 'not subjected in the course of his duty to exceptional exposure'. He was diagnosed as 'sick, debility' and transferred to a special hospital. Tellingly, written on his conduct sheet were the words 'shell shock' as if this was indication of bad behaviour.

By summer 1918 Thomas was on active service again and on the 17th June he was kicked in the jaw by a mule. His jaw was fractured in several places and he lost teeth which were removed by a dentist. He was gradually transferred home, via the Stationary New Zealand hospital in Wisques, France and the 3rd Canadian Hospital in Boulogne, to the Burdon Military Hospital in Weymouth.

His pension records show that he was discharged to the Reserves in March 1919. He was transferred back to Sheffield and he died in Wharncliffe War Hospital on 13 November 1919 of valvular disease of the heart and cerebral embolism.

More telling than these bare facts is the obituary in a Sheffield newspaper:

> Blown up at Passchendaele
>
> The death took place at Wharncliffe War Hospital, Sheffield of Private Thomas Robert Peck of 360 Gleadless Road, who was in the 1/4th (Hallamshires) York and Lancaster Regiment. Blown up during an attack at Passchendaele, he was very badly injured. He went into hospital at Weymouth and remained there for seven months and was then sent to Westcliffe. On the 1st March this year he was demobilised but only worked three days and had to go into hospital again. He had been at Wharncliffe since 11th August. About six weeks ago he had a stroke, and a second last Thursday had a fatal termination. He was the brother of RQMS Peck who was for a long period one of the best known non-commissioned officers in the Hallamshires. Private Peck leaves a widow and two children.

Thomas obviously suffered greatly from the results of his experiences in France. On his funeral card is the sad verse which sums up this torment:

> Long days and nights he lived in pain
> To seek a cure was all in vain;
> For God above
> He thought it best his pain to ease
> And give him rest.

Soldiers commemorated in the General Cemetery

Many of the men whose bodies were never found, or who were buried in the countries where they died, are commemorated on the now lost grave stones in the Anglican section of Sheffield General Cemetery. There is not space here to tell everyone's story but every serviceman commemorated in the Cemetery is recorded in the alphabetical list in the Index at the end of this book. Details of the memorial inscriptions (MIs) and information on all the men listed can be found in the records of the Sheffield General Cemetery Trust.

The men detailed in this chapter are listed in date order according to each one's date of death and this emphasises peaks of activity as, for example, around the Battle of the Somme in July 1916.

1914

Edwin Marsden

The first time the British, supporting the French, faced the German Army in a major action was at Mons. The plan was to prevent the German advance by holding the line on the Mons Canal. Twelve bridges had to be destroyed. Corporal Edwin Marsden Royal Engineers, 17th Field Company, blew up one of these, which cost him his life. He was the son

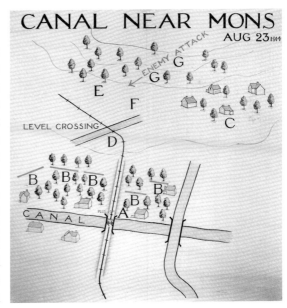

Diagram of canal at Mons

of Arthur Edwin and Sarah Marsden, the son and grandson of carvers of staghorn handles who were also ivory dealers, and had one sister, Ruth. He was educated at Worksop College, served with the Royal Engineers (RE) for seven years, and was an instructor in bridge building. He also invented an improvement to the Wheldon Trestle used in bridge building, known as the Marsden Band Trestle, which was accepted by the War Office.

The family lived first in Cemetery Road but then moved to Hathersage and later to Totley. Edwin's grandfather, whose name he shared, lived in Clarkegrove Road. The MI on the family grave states that Edwin died at St Ghislain, Mons 23rd Aug 1914.

His death was reported in The Times 19th Sept 1914:

> News has reached Sheffield of the death in action of Corporal Edwin Marsden R.E. In a letter conveying news of his death, Major CW Singer, commanding the 17th company, R.E., paid a tribute to his heroism.

> 'It will be a gratification to you' he writes to Corporal Marsden's father, 'to know that he died as he had lived, as a brave soldier and a gentleman. He had just performed a most gallant deed in volunteering to blow up a bridge under very heavy fire, which he did unscathed; shortly afterwards he was hit on the head by a shrapnel bullet and expired instantaneously, without any pain... Personally I feel I have lost a friend and a gallant comrade.'

The Cuthbertian, the newsletter of Edwin's old school, published the same letter with a brief biography, but also included an account written by a private in the Middlesex Regiment to his own family. It had been previously published in the High Peak News and was expressed more bluntly:

> If they [the Germans] had only got across that night, I am afraid there would have been very few of the Middlesex left. The only bridge that was left open to them was blown up by a sergeant [sic] of the Engineers, and the very next moment his own head was carried away by a German shell. But the brave fellow saved the position.

It is noticeable how many of the letters written by officers refer to men dying instantly, without pain – although in this case it was clearly the actual fact. His death was followed by the retreat of the British Expeditionary Force, pursued by the much larger German force.

Mentioned in despatches for gallant or meritorious action in the face of the enemy, Edwin Marsden is buried in Hautrage Military Cemetery near St Ghislain in Hainault, Belgium.

William Mann

Shipping was also vulnerable to attack so armed cruisers were deployed to patrol the North Sea. The HMS Aboukir, along with HMS Cressy and HMS Hogue, were three such. They were, however, comparatively old, and not very well armed. As a result, they were nicknamed 'the live bait squadron'. In fact, Winston Churchill, First Lord of Admiralty, had ordered that they be

HMS Aboukir

withdrawn as the risk outweighed their possible usefulness. The order had not been implemented when a week later, on 22nd September 1914, all three ships were torpedoed and sunk within an hour by a small German U-boat,

U-9, manned by a crew of 30. Approximately 1,400 men died and Sergeant William Horace Mann, Royal Marine Light Infantry, on board the Aboukir, the first attacked, was one of those lost. He was born in Edmonton, London and lived near Chatham with his wife and children but had grown up in Sheffield, where his parents and siblings were still living when war was declared. He had enlisted at the age of 16. According to the Sheffield Evening Telegraph 28th September 1914:

> Mr Charles Mann, draper, of 575 Abbeydale Road, Sheffield, has a son on the Aboukir – William Mann, a sergeant in the Royal Marines. He completed 12 years' service in June last, and 'signed on' for a further period of 9 years. He celebrated his 29th birthday in Sheffield in June, when his holiday was curtailed in view of the mobilisation for manoeuvres, and he was on the Aboukir when war was declared. The cruiser put into Chatham only a week ago for repairs, but these only occupied a few days, and the Aboukir proceeded to sea again. Sergeant Mann is married and has two young children.

A number of reports appeared in the newspapers, all quoting eyewitness accounts of the discipline and courage of the doomed men. Even the captain of U-9, Otto Weddigen, in a published account of what happened when the torpedo struck, commented on this:

> [I] discovered that the shot had gone straight and true, striking the ship, which I later learned was the Aboukir, under one of her magazines, which in exploding helped the torpedo's work of destruction.

> There was a fountain of water, a burst of smoke, a flash of fire, and part of the cruiser rose in the air. Then I heard a roar and felt reverberations sent through the water by the detonation. She had been broken apart and sank in a few minutes. The Aboukir had been stricken in a vital spot and by an unseen force; that made the blow all the greater.

> Her crew were brave, and even with death staring them in the face kept to their posts, ready to handle their useless guns, for I submerged at once. But I had stayed on top long enough to

see the other cruisers, which I learned were the Cressy and the Hogue, turn and steam full speed to their dying sister, whose plight they could not understand….' (from A Memoir of the Sinking of the Aboukir, Cressy and Hogue by U-boat U-9 in September 1914 by Lieutenant Otto Weddigen).

Otto Weddigen was awarded the Iron Cross for his feat in sinking the three ships but died in March 1915 when his U-boat was rammed by the HMS Dreadnought.

William Mann's body was not recovered. He is commemorated in this Cemetery and on the Chatham War Memorial.

1915

Walter Henry Grady

More than 54,000 missing British and Commonwealth servicemen are memorialised on the Ypres (Menin Gate) Memorial in Belgium, sited on the route taken by soldiers on their way to the battlefield. Second Lieutenant Walter Henry Grady, Royal Fusiliers, 6th Battalion, was killed aged 28 on 25th April 1915, the date taken to indicate the start of the second battle of Ypres. He is commemorated on the family grave with the words 'killed in action at Zonnebeke' and on the Ypres (Menin Gate) Memorial. The son of an edge tool manufacturer and

Walter Grady

one of a large family (he had four older sisters and two younger brothers), in 1911 he had been working as a metallurgical chemist in Sheffield, and just before the war he moved to London to set up in business with his brother. In 1912 he married Ida Bateman. Having been a member of Sheffield University Officer Training Corps, he was offered a commission at the start of war which he accepted. He arrived in France on 15th March, a little over a month before he died.

Menin Gate Memorial

Ralph L. Hinde

Sergeant Ralph L Hinde, Northamptonshire Regiment, 1st Battalion, is commemorated on his brother's family grave and on Le Touret Memorial, one of 13,000 British soldiers killed in this section of the Western Front. He was an experienced soldier, already in uniform at the age of 18, by which time his mother Lydia had died and his father John, a blacksmith near Bedford, had remarried. By 1911 however Ralph had left the army and was living with his wife Annie and their three-year-old daughter in Broomhill. Ralph was working as a 'jobbing gardener', perhaps for his older brother Harry who is listed as being a self employed gardening contractor and living in Washington Road. In 1914 Ralph would still be on the reserve list and so would have been immediately called up. According to the Forces War Records he was 'mentioned in despatches'. He died in the Battle of Aubers Ridge on 9th May 1915 aged 31, part of a major offensive. He may have been one of the 560 men of his regiment who went over the top in the first wave following extensive bombardment. Many were cut down by machine gun fire within yards of their own front line trench. Overall more than 11,000 casualties were sustained on 9th May 1915.

Albert Edward Gautier

Albert Edward Gautier, is commemorated on the family grave stone, the second of his family to die in the war. The eldest of four brothers he was just 17 when he enlisted, one of approximately 250,000 boy soldiers who served in the war. He was under age - a recruit was supposed to be 18 to enlist, or 19 to be sent overseas. Albert gave his age as 19 years and one month; birth certificates were not required and it was not an offence under military law to lie about one's age. The pressure to join must have been overwhelming for adventurous boys who, fired by patriotic fervour, knew nothing of what awaited them. The War Office, desperate for men, turned a blind eye. While he remained in the United Kingdom his parents could have asked for his return by providing evidence of his true age but this didn't happen or was not successful. Five foot six inches tall, weighing 119 pounds, he was attested in February 1915, posted with the York and Lancs 1st Battalion on 1st May 1915, in the field in France by 6th June, and listed as killed in action 9 August 1915 at Ypres.

In June he also had to suffer three days of Field Punishment No. 2, which involved spending up to two hours a day in fetters with hard labour and loss of pay. Albert had, according to his service papers, been late for 7.30 tattoo.

Albert Edward is buried at Kemmel Chateau Cemetery, Belgium. For Edna there was further tragedy when her third son Wilfred was accidentally killed during training with the West Yorkshire Regiment in 1921. He was 16 years old and is commemorated on the War Memorial in Sheffield General Cemetery.

Ypres

The First Day of the Somme 1st July 1916

Fourteen of the commemorated men died on the first day of the battle of the Somme or from wounds received on that day. Nine of those were from the 12th (or City) Battalion York and Lancaster Regiment who died near the village of Serre, where today there is a memorial to the men of the City Battalion.

Thiepval Memorial

Harold Brooke Forsdike

Lieutenant Harold Brooke Forsdike was one of the many who had joined Pals Battalions, in this case 2nd Barnsley Pals, York and Lancs 14th Battalion, and died with them on the first day of the Battle of the Somme, 1st July 1916. One of six brothers, he was the son of William Forsdike, listed in White's Directory for 1913 as 'W. & A. Forsdike Limited, joiners, builders, contractors, painters, glaziers and gasfitters, 24-32 St Mary's Road; 379 Queens Road and 151 Young Street.' He had a comparatively privileged upbringing: in 1911, aged 15, Harold is at boarding school in Blackpool with his brother Leonard, 16. The Sheffield Independent 8th July 1916 reported his death, quoting from the letter sent to his father:

Harold Forsdike

He was a splendid officer and did his duty fearlessly and you will be proud to know that he met his death as an officer and a gentleman.

The article also quoted from Leonard's letter. He had been there too, and tried to soften the blow:

As to Harold, nobody really knows that he has been killed. As soon as I could get away I set about to find him, or to get news of him, and in the end rode over to see the colonel. All the news I got was that he was last seen to jump into the German trench. All his men were shot down except one, who landed with Harold at the German line. This man was then wounded and saw Harold go into the trench. What happened to him afterwards I cannot say. In any case, I am very proud of him, and I hope you will be, for nobody knows what we all went through, and the magnificent way he led his men over open ground.

His body was never found: he is commemorated on Thiepval Memorial. Leonard and four other brothers survived the war.

Forsdike family grave

George Charles Hastings

Private George Charles Hastings, York and Lancs Regiment, 9th Battalion, was listed as 'wounded and missing' 1.7.16 aged 25. One of a family of five brothers and four sisters, he married when he was 18 and his wife 16, and by 1911 they had a baby daughter. George followed his father's trade and was an 'ashfalter's labourer' - perhaps working with his father. Five feet four inches tall and weighing 119 lbs, he enlisted in October 1914. In 1916 his son, also George, died aged 2 of mastoiditis and pneumonia. The War Office immediately reduced the allowance paid to his wife. A third child, a daughter, was born the same year. After his death the only possession found that could be sent to Mary, who remarried in 1917, was his identity disc. Later she received his 1914-15 Star. He is buried in Blighty Valley Cemetery, Authuille Wood and is commemorated on the grave of George Hatfield along with a brother born after his death.

William Stanley Meeke

One of four siblings, Captain William Stanley Meeke, Middlesex Regiment, 2nd Battalion, was the second son of Joseph Meeke, linen draper at 64 Snig Hill until his death in 1912. The eldest, Raymond, was a solicitor and William had qualified as a barrister at law with an address in London by 1911. Raymond and a younger brother survived the war, but William died 1st July 1916 at La Boiselle, aged 28, perhaps one of those caught in machine gunfire from Ovillers and La Boiselle. The battalion suffered 650 casualties that day. According to the Sheffield Evening Telegraph, 17 October 1916, William S. Meeke had been awarded the Military Cross and mentioned in despatches. William is commemorated on the Meeke family grave and is buried in Ovillers Military Cemetery.

Harold and Rowland Norris

Private Harold Norris, York and Lancs, 12th Battalion, was the eldest of the two sons and two daughters of Sarah H and James Norris, a commission agent. Both sons died. In 1911 Harold was a cabinet maker but he was killed aged 26 on 1.7.1916. He is buried in the Railway Hollow Cemetery, Hauterne.

Harold Norris

His younger brother, Private Rowland Norris, Kings Own, (Royal Lancaster Regiment) 9th Battalion, formerly Royal Army Medical Corps, went missing in Salonika and was presumed dead 19 September 1918 aged 21. His battalion was involved in the failed allied attack on Bulgarian positions in the Battle of Doiran 18-19 September. He was mourned not only by his family at 11 Ward Place but also by his fiancée Winnie who lived at 11 Violet Bank Road. He is commemorated on the Doiran Memorial, Greece, and like his brother, on the family grave in the General Cemetery.

Herbert and Maurice Barber

Herbert Barber, who in 1909 was Master Cutler, also lost two sons yet in 1910 he must have felt that he had all a man could desire. He was one of the directors of the very successful steel manufacturer, Daniel Doncaster and Sons, having entered the firm as a 17-year-old. Two of his sisters had married grandsons of the founder, and by 1910 he had himself been a director of the firm for many years. Of his five children, two had died very young but he had a beautiful and admired wife, three sons to carry on his traditions, and a comfortable life style. Two sons also joined the firm and became directors. Then war came. Although they were a Quaker family,

Herbert Barber

as were the Doncasters, the brothers enlisted. Isabel died in 1915 and so was spared the grief of hearing that her eldest son, Captain Herbert Graham Barber, York and Lancs, 4th Battalion, had been killed in action on the Somme 7th July 1916. The Yorkshire Post and Leeds Intelligencer 13 July 1916 reported that:

> Capt. Herbert Graham Barber …was a favourite officer with the York and Lancasters, and devoted to his duties, having recently been awarded the Military Cross.

An officer wrote that

> 'From an easy going and charming comrade, he became a most enthusiastic soldier and leader without sacrificing any of his charming nature. He was always thinking of his men…' and the

commanding officer of the 49th West Riding Division wrote 'he was an excellent officer in every respect, not only very gallant under fire, but a fine example to those under him at all times. Everything he had to do seems to have been well done. I have never had better reports on any officer.'

Sheffield Evening Telegraph 12 July 1916 noted:

Many of the correspondents who have written on 'the great push' of the Ist July have referred to the remarkable work done by York and Lancaster Battalions and East Lancashire men. The former includes hundreds of men from Sheffield and district, and unfortunately many have been killed and wounded. But General O'Gowan says 'it was worth it'. A letter from this distinguished military officer was read by the Lord Mayor at the annual meeting of the Sheffield YMCA at which the Princess Victoria Helena was present yesterday. The General wrote: 'I am certain you will be interested to know how well the York and Lancaster Brigade fought on Saturday last (July 1st). All the battalions and many of the men of the East Lancashires distinguished themselves by their coolness, dash and extraordinary bravery. Their advance in the face of a terrific bombardment was beyond all praise, and one of the finest performances ever accomplished by British soldiers. I am sure Yorkshire and Lancashire will appreciate the way the whole Division behaved'.

The newspaper went on to report:

Deep sympathy will be extended to Mr Herbert Barber of Oakhurst, Manchester Road, Sheffield, ex Master Cutler, who this morning received the sad news that his son Captain Herbert Graham Barber, has been killed. Captain Barber was 31 years of age, and was educated at Leighton Park School, Reading. He entered the firm of Messrs Daniel Doncaster and Sons in 1903 and became a director in 1909. He was awarded the Military Cross recently.

Herbert is commemorated on the family grave and buried in Authuile Military Cemetery.

Eighteen months later Herbert junior's younger brother, Captain Maurice Barber, York and Lancs, 2nd/4th Battalion, died 26 November 1917 age 25. The Yorkshire Post and Leeds Intelligencer 5 December 1917 reported that he too entered the firm of Daniel Doncaster and Sons in 1914 before enlisting in the same year. At the time of his death, he was adjutant to his regiment.

Mentioned in despatches, he is commemorated on the family grave with his brother and on the Cambrai Memorial, Louverval. The youngest brother died in 1929.

Memorial board at Sheffield Cathedral

Ernest R. Shuttleworth

Second Lieutenant Ernest R Shuttleworth, Royal Warwickshire Regiment, the eldest of the three sons of Thomas and Mary Shuttleworth, also died 1 July 1916 age 22. He, like his brother Kenneth, was first in the Public

The Somme

Shuttleworth family grave

Schools Battalion. Ernest enlisted 30 November 1914 and both brothers served in the RNVR. On 26 April 1915 Ernest was discharged to commission as Second Lieutenant, Royal Warwickshire Regiment. A few months after Ernest's death, Kenneth was discharged, invalided out with sciatic neuritis. Their father and grandfather were both chartered accountants, and in the 1911 census Ernest is described as a student. Ernest is commemorated on his family grave and on the Thiepval Memorial.

Charles Henry Wardill

Charles Wardill

Second Lieutenant Charles Henry Wardill, York and Lancs 15th Battalion, was attached to the 12th Battalion when he died 1 July 1916 aged 39. He was married and had no children but was the eldest of six brothers and three sisters. In 1901 he was a cutlery warehouse salesman and in 1911 a commercial traveller. Tragically his brother Sydney who was in the York and Lancs 12th Battalion, and married with two daughters, also died that day. Charles is commemorated on the family grave, and both Charles and Sydney on the Thiepval Memorial.

Bernard Walter Davy

Midshipman Bernard Walter Davy Royal Naval Reserve, HMS Ark Royal, and attached to the Royal Naval Air Service, was killed aged 21 whilst flying as an observer on 10 July 1916 at Imbros, Gallipoli Peninsula. The son of a steel works manager who was living in Dover Road in 1911, he had been mentioned in despatches. He is commemorated on the family grave and is buried in the Lancashire Landing Cemetery in Turkey.

Norman Percy Burrell

Private Norman Percy Burrell, York and Lancs, 2nd Battalion, who died aged 19, was an only child. His was a protected occupation but he wanted to volunteer. His death was reported in the Sheffield Independent, 5 August 1916:

Killed in France on 20th July, having been there little over a fortnight.

Employed at the works of Messrs Edgar Allen & Co Ltd, he obtained permission to enlist last February and joined the City Battalion. He was keen on all types of sport and as a member of the Audrey Tennis Club displayed great promise. A comrade writes from the heart: 'It is very sad. He was so well liked by all of us and everybody speaks of it with regret'.

Norman Percy Burrell

He is commemorated on his grandparents' grave and buried in Authuile Military Cemetery, five km north of Albert.

Harold Edward Dyson

Second Lieutenant Harold Edward Dyson, York and Lancs, 4th (Hallamshire) Battalion (Territorial), the youngest son of Henry, a steel merchant, and Hannah Dyson, died 31 July 1916 aged 23.

The Sheffield Evening Telegraph reported his death on 7 August 1916:

Toll of War.

News has been received from the War Office of the death of Second Lieutenant Harold Dyson of a local battalion of the York and Lancs Regiment. Lieutenant Dyson, who was killed in action on August 1st, was the youngest son of Mr and Mrs Henry Dyson of Cowlishaw Road, Sheffield. He joined the army shortly after the outbreak of war, and was granted a commission on December 20th, 1914. He was educated at Wesley College, Sheffield, and Oakham School, Rutland, and was engaged prior to the war at the Union of London and Smiths Bank, High Street. Lieutenant Dyson's Commanding Officer writes:

'He, with two other officers, was in a dugout which had a direct hit by a heavy shell, which killed all three. They must have been killed instantaneously and so had no suffering. Your boy was a charming companion, and a splendid officer, loved by all who knew him. His death is a great loss to me personally and also to the regiment. '

He is commemorated on the Dyson family grave and buried in Blighty Valley Cemetery, Authuille Wood.

The administration of Harold's will was granted to 'Phyllis Robinson, spinster'. Phyllis was the daughter of a steel merchant and 21 in 1916. Perhaps they had hoped to marry.

Henry and Abel Martin

The parents of Private Henry Martin, York and Lancs, 8th Battalion, and Gunner Abel Martin, Royal Field Artillery, 81st Battalion, lived in Exeter originally where the father worked as a bricklayer, but after their first child was born in 1871 they moved to Sheffield where another 12 children were born. By 1911 three children had died and the remaining children had all left home. Henry married Ada Ann Bradwell in 1898 and had two sons, Harold and James. He worked as a jobbing bricklayer and in 1911 lived in Norton.

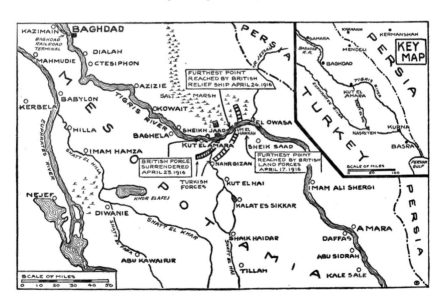

Map showing location of Kut

It is not known when he enlisted but he was killed in action aged 37 on 6th September 1916 at Albert, according to the monumental inscription in the General Cemetery, and is buried in Contalmaison Chateau Cemetery. His family can barely have been informed of Henry's death when his brother Abel, already a regular soldier in 1911, died 5 October 1916 aged 26, a prisoner of war in Turkey following the surrender of Kut. Men captured suffered an appalling fate: prisoners were routinely starved and beaten during the march from Kut to Baghdad. Abel probably died on the march or in one of the labour camps, having survived six months as a prisoner.

The youngest child of James and Rosina, he is buried in Baghdad (North Gate) War Cemetery, many bodies having been brought in from the surrounding areas. He is also commemorated on the Martin family grave.

Albert Edward Jay

Private Albert Edward Jay, KOYLI, 6th Battalion, was a clerk with a silversmith in 1911 and married by the time of his death. After four months in the field he received gunshot wounds to the chest and right arm and was taken by ambulance train to No 34 Casualty Clearing Station where he died aged 23 on 21st September 1916. One of two sons, his older brother survived the war living until 1944. Albert is commemorated on the Foster family grave and buried in St Sever Cemetery, Rouen.

William Crossland

Private William Ernest Gladstone Crossland, York and Lancs Regiment, 2nd Battalion, was killed in action 14th March 1916 aged 31 and is buried in Menin Road South Military Cemetery. Because he was a Class 1 National Reservist, having previously been in the Coldstream Guards, he was one of the first to be called up despite the fact that he had been recently widowed - his wife died in 1913 - and had three small children, William, Margaret and Agnes, the latter named after his wife. He left them in the guardianship of his mother Rebecca, and his 1914-15 star was sent to her as next of kin. A pension of 15 shillings a week was awarded to the children from October 1916. However, William's mother died and correspondence among his military service papers suggests that the authorities then asked for the medal to be returned until the children's new guardian could be confirmed. William was the eldest of 5 children. Two had died by 1911. It fell to his sister Edith

Ellen, known as Nellie, and three years younger than himself, to assume responsibility for the children. Their younger brother Harold, 17 in 1920, was living with William's grandparents. A letter from William's sister signed 'yours respectfully' sounds somewhat exasperated and certainly reproachful:

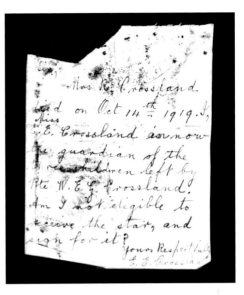

Letter from Edith Crossland

> Mrs R. Crossland died in 1919. I, E. Crossland, am now the guardian of the three children left by Pte W.E.G. Crossland. Am I not eligible to receive the star and sign for it?

William is commemorated on the Crossland family grave and buried in the Menin Road South Military Cemetery.

George Burch

Private George Burch, Cameronians (Scottish Rifles) Ist Battalion, formerly York and Lancs, was killed in action aged 24 on 19 December 1916. He was the grandson of Alderman Thomas Edward Burch, who had traded as a plumbing and decorating contractor under his original name of Mycock, at 108 Barkers Pool. George's father, Henry Herbert, lived on his own means; it is not known what work George did before enlisting. He is commemorated on the family grave as 'Lance Corporal George Burch' and is buried in Hem Farm Military Cemetery, Hem-Monacu. George was the eldest of his father's family with his second wife. One of his younger brothers, Norman, a butcher, trained as a transport driver in the Royal Army Service Corps and was posted to Salonika. He survived the war.

1917

Edwin Mossforth Doughty

Pioneer Edwin Mossforth Doughty, Royal Engineers 'M' Company, No 3 Special Railway Battalion, was, as the name suggests, involved in laying track to get supplies as close as possible to the front line. He was caught in

Building a railway track

a gas attack and died 1st March 1917 aged 21. The eldest of seven children, he was born and brought up in Barnsley although by 1915 the family had moved to 33 Clarkehouse Road, Sheffield. Edwin's father was a non-denominational minister, and in 1911 the family had 4 servants, a nurse and nursemaid, a housemaid and a cook. It was the task of the next of kin to sign for the receipt of the dead serviceman's possessions and Edwin had been well equipped. As well as letters, photos, a bible and hymn book, he had a watch and chain, cigarettes and holder, a pipe, penknife scissors, a book, a notebook, a pencil and a diary. He is buried in Ecoivres Military Cemetery and commemorated on the family grave. A younger brother also joined up, but survived the war.

John Norris Eaton

John Norris Eaton

Lieutenant John Norris Eaton, Canadian Infantry, 43rd Battalion, died 5th April 1917 age 20. The middle one of three sons, he had emigrated with his family from Dore to Calgary, Canada, at some point after 1901 where his father was a solicitor. John went to Bishop Pinkham's College where he was considered a natural leader, becoming head boy, and at the time of his enlistment in April 1916 he was studying law. He had had some military experience as a member of the Calgary Rifles and was given the position of Lieutenant. He was one of the well trained Canadians attacking Vimy Ridge and according to one source was shot in the head by a German sniper while covering a raiding party. He is buried Ecoivres Military Cemetery, Mont-St. Eloi (plots V and VI contain the graves of men killed in the capture of Vimy Ridge in April 1917) and commemorated on his grandparents' grave. Bishop Pinkham College also erected a tablet in his honour on the wall of the Pro-Cathedral Church of the Redeemer. It was unveiled by the Lord Bishop of Calgary and reads:

> To the glory of God and in memory of Lieut. John Norris Eaton, who was killed in action at Vimy Ridge, April 5, 1917. Fidelis ad Finem. Erected by his friends and schoolfellows at the Bishop Pinkham College.

Alfred John and Douglas Honer

Private Alfred John Honer, Cameronians (Scottish Rifles), died eight days into the second Battle of Arras on 14 April 1917 age 20. One of four children of a Royal Navy gunner, he is commemorated on the Arras Memorial, one of 35,000 servicemen from the U.K., South Africa and New Zealand who died in this sector from 1916 to August 1917. Alfred's older brother, Lieutenant Douglas James Honer, Royal Flying Corps, 55th Royal Field Artillery, was an engineering student in 1911. He was killed in action a little more than two months after Alfred, on 4 June 1917 aged 25. The average flying life of a pilot in April 1917 was 18 hours and between the 4th

Arras Flying Memorial

and 8th of April, 75 aircraft and 105 crew were lost in combat. Parachutes were not issued until 1918.

Douglas is commemorated on the Arras Flying Memorial. The brothers are also commemorated on the family grave. Their father, William, in the Royal Navy, survived the war.

Neither brother has any known grave.

Fred Barnes

Lance Corporal Fred Barnes, Kings Royal Rifle Corps, 11th Battalion, had been a spoon and fork filer but had volunteered 3 September 1914, when

Casualty clearing station

he was 21. His father had died in 1908 and his eldest brother in 1914, and Fred lived with his mother Alice at 29 Egerton Street. The youngest of a family of three boys and four girls, he was 5 foot 4 inches tall, 116 lbs and had green eyes. He had about a year's training before embarking for France July 1st 1915 and completed two years' active service before dying of wounds aged 24, probably in the 34th Casualty Clearing Station at La Chapelette, on 8 May 1917. In his service record there is a note from his widowed mother acknowledging receipt of her son's personal belongings on 6 August 1917. Not all items are legible but there is a watch, notebooks, a 9 carat gold ring, a wallet, photograph, cards and a case. Fred is commemorated on the family grave and buried in La Chapelette British and Indian Cemetery, Peronne.

George and Albert Smith

Private George William Smith, York and Lancs Regiment, 14th Battalion, died of wounds on 31 May 1917 in a Stationary Hospital aged 29. George had an abdominal wound and suspected diphtheria and was probably brought by train from the front to Etaples, which had a number of hospitals. A nurse, Elsie Tranter, who was working at 46 Stationary Hospital at the time, wrote in her diary on 2nd May:

> We see the most ghastly wounds and are all day long inhaling the odour of gas gangrene. How these boys suffer. This war is absolute hell. We see and hear, all day and every day, the results of its frightfulness. We can hear the guns quite plainly here.

A housepainter in 1911, he was married with two sons. In November of 1917 his wife Alice was awarded a pension of 22s 6d for herself and her children effective from 3 December 1917. George was buried in Etaples Military Cemetery. He was one of the two sons and three daughters of George and Emma Clementina Smith who lived at 45 Sherrington Road, Sheffield and is commemorated on his parents' grave, along with his younger brother, Private Albert Ernest Smith, West Yorkshire Regiment (Prince of Wales Own), 11th Battalion. Albert was killed in action a week later, on 7 June 1917 aged 27 and is commemorated on the Ypres (Menin Gate) Memorial.

James Cyril Ecclestone

Private James Cyril Ecclestone, KOYLI, 1st/4th Battalion, died from gas poisoning 25 July 1917 aged 21. He was the youngest child and only son of James and Ann Ecclestone and in 1911, aged 14, was a wireworker. He was buried in Mont Huon Military Cemetery, Le Treport, which was the location of at least five hospitals during World War I. He is also commemorated on his family plot.

Three days after his death, his parents placed a death notice in Sheffield Evening Telegraph (28 July 1917):

> Eccleston – In loving memory of Private J.C. Eccleston, KOYLI, died in hospital, in France, July25th, 1917 from gas poisoning, in his 21st year, dearly loved and only son of James E and Annie Eccleston, 329 Glossop Rd, Sheffield.
>
> The unknown grave is the bitterest blow,
>
> None but an aching heart can know.
>
> From Mother, Father, Sisters, Brother in law and Aunts E and C.

Laurence Whiteley

Lieutenant Laurence Whiteley, Black Watch (Royal Highlanders), 5th Battalion (Angus and Dundee,) died 31 July 1917 aged 32. He is commemorated on the Whiteley family grave and on the Spanish Memorial, Wieltje Farm Cemetery. The son of Annie Elizabeth and Seth, principal of Whiteley's Commercial College in Surrey Street, and living at 30 Collegiate Crescent, Sheffield, Laurence had an MA in mathematics and classics from Durham University. From 1907 he was vice principal of Whiteley's College where his two older sisters worked as assistant teachers. When war was declared he was

Laurence Whiteley

keen to enlist but was rejected a number of times because of poor eyesight. He persevered, had new glasses made, and was finally able to enlist with Royal Sussex Regiment in December 1914 as a private before gaining a commission with the Black Watch. In December 1916 he was drafted to France, seconded to a machine gun company and, three months before he was killed, gained his full lieutenancy.

Maurice Nicholson

Second Lieutenant Maurice Nicholson, Royal Flying Corps, 11th Squadron, and General List Army Cyclist Corps, died 18 August 1917 aged 30. He was the second eldest surviving son of Richard Nicholson, who had taken over the management of John Nicholson and Sons steel works, after his own father, James, died in 1909. The Sheffield Independent for 25 August 1917, reporting that Maurice was missing, explained that before the war he had trained in London to become a mining engineer:

Maurice Nicholson

> He joined the OTC at the University of Sheffield and was given a commission in the Norfolk Regiment, from which he was transferred to the Army Cyclists Corps, and was made adjutant in a school of gunnery. He volunteered for the RFC and went to France in 1915.

Three days after returning from a fortnight's leave, he made his last flight. Maurice is commemorated on the family grave as having died 'in aerial combat over France' and on the Arras Flying Services Memorial.

Walter L. Giddy

Private Walter L. Giddy, KOYLI, 1st/5th Battalion, was the son of William Henry Giddy, a joiner from Cornwall, and his wife Sarah Ellen. They had had six children but by 1911 four of them had died and William was a widower. Walter, also a joiner, married Florence that year but was killed 9 October, 1917 aged 31. He had been wounded and was suffering from shell shock in July after a year of service and 7 months in the field but was discharged back to duty on 5 August. He is commemorated on the family grave and on the Tyne Cot Memorial, his body not having been found.

King's Own Yorkshire Light Infantry cap badge

Leonard Staley

Private Leonard Staley, Duke of Wellington's (West Riding) Regiment, 2nd/6th Battalion, was killed in action in France 27th November 1917 when his battalion was engaged in the battle of Cambrai. He was aged 30. He was one of the seven children of William, a 'spade, fork worker' and Mary Ann Staley. In 1911 Leonard was a wooden rule maker and the following year he married Edith Hill in Sheffield. But Edith died in January 1917, according to the MI, and is buried in Huddersfield. Their only child, Kathleen, died in 1931 aged 17 years and 11 months, and is buried in the family grave. Leonard is commemorated on the same grave and on Cambrai Memorial, Louverval.

1918

Graham Mannifield

The son of Graham and Mary Mannifield, in 1901 Private Graham Mannifield, KOYLI, 2/5th Battalion, was living at 89 South View Road with his mother, two older sisters and a younger brother. He was one of 12 siblings, but two older brothers died in infancy. His father, also Graham, had died in 1897 and by 1911 Mary and three of her children, including Graham, were at the same address but with Ernest Mannifield, whom Mary had married two years earlier. He was a 'table knife hafter' as were Graham and his younger brother, Leonard. In 1912 Graham married Ethel Pashley and later had a daughter, Elsie. He was killed in action aged 30 on 1 February 1918 in France and is buried in Roclincourt Military Cemetery which was used as a front line cemetery until October 1918. He is commemorated on the family grave. Leonard also enlisted in 1916, joining the Royal Garrison Artillery, and although wounded in 1917, survived to return to the front and later to his wife Nellie, who lived in Lansdowne Road during the war. Leonard died in 1961.

Edward Shemeld

Private Edward Shemeld, York and Lancs Regiment, Machine Gun Corps (Infantry) 31st Company, died 30th March 1918 aged 29. He was awarded the Military Medal, which was for 'acts of gallantry and devotion to duty under fire or for individual or associated acts of bravery' for those below commissioned rank – the other ranks' equivalent of the Military Cross. One of 11 children, he had been a spoon and fork filer, marrying

Military Medal

May in 1909. A daughter, Vera May, was born in 1910. By the time he died he had at least one other child. Two In Memoriam notices appeared in the Sheffield Evening Telegraph 26 March 1919, one from his parents, giving the information that he had been killed by a sniper, and one from his wife, giving their address as 53 Coniston Road. He is commemorated on his paternal grandparents' grave, with the words, 'Well done, thou good and faithful servant', and also on the Arras Memorial.

Henry Hunter

Private Henry Hunter, East Yorkshire Regiment, 11th Battalion, was killed in action on 12 April 1918 aged 24. A spoon and fork stamper, working at Deakin's silversmiths and electro platers, he had volunteered in Sept 1914, and had spent two periods in hospital in 1915 recovering from shrapnel wounds to his right arm, thigh and foot. Even when discharged in the November of 1915, he was still limping. The month following his death, a notice appeared in the Sheffield Evening Telegraph on 4th May 1918:

> Hunter – Private H. Hunter, of the East Yorkshire Regiment, killed in action on April 12th, aged 24 years. He joined the

colours on September 4th 1914, from the firm of Deakin's, Matilda Street, Sheffield, and was also a member of Mount Tabor Bible Class. Nearer my God to Thee

From his sorrowing Father, Mother, Sisters, Brothers and Brothers-in-law.

For Henry's parents, 1918 was a particularly tragic year because a second son and a daughter also died. Two sons and a daughter survived the war years. Henry is commemorated on the family grave, and on the Ploegsteert Memorial, Belgium along with 11,000 UK and South African servicemen. The CWGC states:

Most of those commemorated by the Memorial did not die in major offensives...... but in the course of day to day trench warfare which characterised this part of the line or in small scale set engagements usually in support of major attacks taking place elsewhere.

The Last Post is still sounded there on the first Friday of every month.

Tom Cyril Sherrick Guy

Private Tom C. S. Guy, York and Lancs Regiment, 7th Battalion, was the only child of Thomas and Maria Guy. In 1911 they lived in Walkley, Thomas working as 'an inspector of steel', and Tom as a piano and organ tuner and repairer. When Tom enlisted in December 1915 he was described as a 'works manager' living at 41 Hawksley Avenue, Hillsborough, Unusually, he was tall, almost 6 foot, but weighing just 128 pounds. He was wounded in October 1917 but patched up and returned to the front where he was killed 27 May 1918, almost 18 months after his father had died. His belongings were sent to his mother - cards, wallet, cigarette case and holder, cap badge and one coin, a farthing. He is buried in Acheux British Cemetery, and he is commemorated on his parents' grave. His mother outlived both husband and son, dying in 1934.

William Redfearn

Private William Redfearn, Machine Gun Corps, 3rd Battalion, was one of the four surviving children of George and Mary Redfearn who were living with their family and a servant at 169 Ecclesall Road in 1911. George was a baker and Jack, William's older brother, a merchant's clerk. There is no occupation listed for William. William died of wounds in the 16th General Hospital Le Treport, France May 22nd 1918, aged 23. He is commemorated on the family grave and buried in Mont Huon Military Cemetery. Jack married in 1915 shortly after enlisting in the Army Service Corps to be trained as a motor transport driver. He survived the war and died in Sheffield.

Branson Saltfleet

Private Branson Saltfleet, York and Lancs Regiment, 2nd Battalion, died 18 October 1918 age 28. He is commemorated on his grandparents' grave and buried in Vadencourt British Cemetery, Maissemy. The only surviving child of William and Mary Saltfleet, he was a housepainter in 1911 following the example of his father and grandfather, and living with his parents at 12 Court, 2 House, Broomhall Street. He married Lily Brooks 15 April 1914 and enlisted December 1915. By the time of his death, he had two children, including a son, also named Branson. In 1920 Lily wrote from his parents' address to ask if someone could tell her what she had to do in order to get a photo of her husband's grave. There is no record of the answer. Branson's mother died in 1933, his father in 1934. Lily did not remarry and was named as the sole beneficiary in her father-in-law's will.

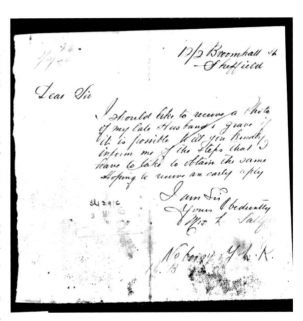

Letter from Lily Saltfleet

Henry Atkinson

Private Henry Atkinson, Devonshire Regiment, 9th Battalion, died 9 November 1918 aged 24. Ironically, having survived shrapnel and gunfire, in the very month that war ceased, he contracted the pneumonia which killed him. The only child of Henry and Mary Ann Atkinson, in 1911 he was a junior office clerk. He is commemorated on his Jennet grandparents' grave, with the words:

> Also of Henry Atkinson, grandson of the above, died in France November 9th, 1918 aged 24 years.
>
> He was just our all.

By this time both grandparents had died so the poignant last words must have been those of his parents.

He is buried in St Sever Cemetery Extension, Rouen, a centre for military hospitals during World War One.

Albert Victor Giles

Private Albert Victor Giles, York and Lancs Regiment, 1/4th Battalion, B Company, was the son of Albert F. and Annie Giles. In 1916 when Albert enlisted he stated that his occupation was 'chemical manufacturer' which suggests that he was working with his father, a successful paint and varnish manufacturer who had premises at 46 West Street. Albert was just five feet tall and weighed one hundred pounds. He was killed in action 12 April 1918, but this was not immediately clear to his family. Scraps of letters with his military service papers suggest that he was at first listed as missing, leaving his family with some hope. Another letter, this time from Albert's father, seems to suggest that one of his fellow soldiers later wrote to them but nothing more. Albert senior was a self-made man, having been born in Somerset and started work as a twine twister; he came from a large family himself but after his son died there was no one to carry on his business. He had one daughter left. Albert Victor's body was never found. He is commemorated on the Tyne Cot Memorial and on his maternal grandparents' gravestone.

Edward S Garwell

Private Edward S. Garwell, East Yorkshire Regiment, C Company, 7th Battalion, was the fourth of the six children of Jesse and Emma Garwell. Jesse and two of his sons were tailors, but in 1911 aged 21 and still living at home at 11 Thirlwell Road, Heeley, Edward was working as a bricklayer. In 1915 Edward's family had moved to 71 Thirwell Road. According to his military record, Edward was 5' 1 3/8" inches tall and weighed 112 lbs. In May 1917 he was briefly admitted to hospital with a sprained ankle which occurred when he was in no man's land 'between Cuba and Charlie trenches'. He was wounded 28 August 1918, dying 21 September 1918, and having probably been treated at one of the hospitals in Le Treport, is buried in Mont Huon Military Cemetery. He is also commemorated on his family grave. His personal effects were sent home in June 1919; his family had to sign for 'letter, pipe, wallet, handkerchief, 2 knives, shaving soap and brush, razor, spectacles in case, watch (broken), 2 cap badges, a shrapnel bullet, numeral and button'. His brothers survived the war.

War ends 11th November 1918

They shall grow not old as we that are left grow old;
Age shall not weary them, nor the years condemn.
At the going down of the sun and in the morning
We will remember them.

Laurence Binyon (1869 - 1943)

Index

Servicemen buried or commemorated in the General Cemetery

All these men have been researched as part of this project and further information on them is available from the Sheffield General Cemetery Trust. Details of all the men buried in the Cemetery and of a representative sample of the commemorated men are included in this book as indicated by the page references.

Private **John Allsop** 17328 York and Lancs Regiment 9th Bn. Died of wounds 12.6.1917 aged 31. Commemorated SGC Noncon Z 15. Buried XV.H.12 Lijssenthoek Military Cemetery. Son of Charles and the late Mary Ann Allsop. Husband of Jane Newbould (formerly Allsop) of Sheffield.

Private **Allan Armstrong** 241731 Highland Light Infantry 9th (Glasgow Hldrs.) Bn. Died of wounds 28.9.1918 aged 21. Buried SGC Anglican H1 127. Son of Mr and Mrs K Armstrong of 22 Ashford Rd, Sharrow, Sheffield. (see page 34)

Chaplain The Rev. **Frederick William Ashton** Attd. Royal Air Force. Died of influenza 18.11.1918 aged 33. Buried SGC Noncon H126. Son of the late William Henry and Lucy Ashton, Devon. (see page 41)

Private **Walter Atkin** 16643 Coldstream Guards 1st Bn. KIA 15.9.16 aged 37. Commemorated SGC Anglican Z2 77. Buried XII.R.8 Guards Cemetery, Lesboeufs. Son of William and Annie Atkin, 25 Spur St, Olive Grove, Sheffield.

Private **Henry Atkinson** 69034 Devonshire Regiment 9th Bn. Died 9.11.18 of pneumonia aged 24. Commemorated SGC Anglican L3 167. Buried St Sever Cemetery, Rouen. Son of Henry and Mary Ann Atkinson of Sheffield. (see page 80)

Private **Joseph Harold Bagshaw** 2075 York and Lancs Regiment 12th Bn.

KIA 24.1.18 aged 23. Commemorated SGC Anglican V1 90. Buried III.F.14 Roclincourt Military Cemetery. Son of Henry and Phoebe Bagshaw of 122 Blair Athol Road, Ecclesall, Sheffield.

Captain **Herbert Graham Barber** York and Lancs 4th Bn. KIA 7.7.16 aged 31. Commemorated SGC Noncon EE 40. Buried in G3 Authuile Military Cemetery. Eldest son of Herbert and Isabel Barber of The Firs, Dore. Military Cross. (see page 61)

Captain **Maurice Barber** York and Lancs Regiment 2nd/4th Bn. KIA 26.11.17 aged 25. Commemorated SGC Noncon EE 40 and Panel 9 and 10 Cambrai Memorial, Louverval. Youngest son of Herbert and Isabel Barber of The Firs, Dore, Sheffield. Mentioned in despatches. (see page 61)

Lance Corporal **Fred Barnes** R/983 Kings Royal Rifle Corps 11th Bn. Died of wounds 8.5.17 aged 24. Commemorated SGC Anglican Y1 82. Buried II.D.11 La Chapelette British and Indian Cemetery, Peronne. Son of Alice Barnes, 29 Egerton St, Sheffield. (see page 72)

Gunner **John Batty** 71527 Royal Horse Artillery and Royal Field Artillery 21st Anti Aircraft Section. KIA 25.9.15 in Mesopotamia. Commemorated SGC Anglican X1 44 and Panel 3 and 60 Basra Memorial in Iraq. Son of Elizabeth Batty of Sheffield.

Private **Bernard Beaumont** 49961 Lincolnshire Regiment 7th Bn. KIA 26.8.18 aged 35. Commemorated SGC Anglican K3 167 and on the Spanish Memorial 44 Warlencourt British Cemetery. Son of John James and Clara Beaumont of Sheffield.

Private **Archibald Benton** 241861 York and Lancs Regiment 2nd/5th Bn. Died of wounds 5.5.17 aged 32. Commemorated SGC Anglican C1 189. Buried II.J.15 Wimereux Communal Cemetery. Son of Charles W. and Matha E. Benton of Sheffield.

Captain **Gilbert Wilson Fitzroy Birch** KOYLI 11th Bn. KIA 24.8.17. Commemorated SGC Noncon AA 59 and Panel 108-111 Tyne Cot Memorial. Son of Gilbert F. and Sarah A. L. Birch of Sheffield.

Private **Edgar Firth Bradbury** 202594 York and Lancs Regiment 2/4th Bn. KIA 3.5.17 aged 25. Commemorated SGC Anglican T2 51 and Bay 8 Arras

Memorial. Son of Joseph and Fanny Bradbury of Sheffield.

Private **Clifton Braithwaite** M/298029 Royal Army Service Corps. Died 9.3.1917 aged 28. Buried SGC Anglican N1 116. Husband of Ada Braithwaite of 13 Edge Hill Rd, Nether Edge, Sheffield. (see page 27)

Private **George Burch** 40974 Cameronians (Scottish Rifles) 1ˢᵗ Bn. KIA 19.12.16 aged 25. Commemorated SGC Anglican W1 76. Buried I.D.3 Hem Farm Military Cemetery, Hem-Monacu. Son of the late Mr and Mrs Henry Herbert Burch of Sheffield. (see page 69)

Private **Norman Percy Burrell** 12/1991 York and Lancs 12ᵗʰ Bn. KIA 20.7.16 aged 19. Commemorated SGC Anglican U1 36 and buried I.10 Authuile Military Cemetery. Only son of Percy and Gertrude Burrell of 10 Byron Rd, Nether Edge, Sheffield. (see page 65)

Private **Charles Cheetham** (served under the name of Charles Foster) T/390690 Royal Army Service Corps. Died 2.2.1919 aged 54. Buried SGC Anglican U89. (see page 44)

Lance Corporal **John Philip Chellingworth** (also recorded as Chillingworth) 16953 Coldstream Guards 4ᵗʰ Bn. Died of wounds 24.11.1916 aged 18. Buried SGC Anglican M1 7. Son of Frederick John and Charlotte Georgina Chellingworth of 29 Kearsley Rd., Highfield, Sheffield. (see page 21)

Private **William E.G. Crossland** 4677 York and Lancs 2ⁿᵈ Bn. KIA 14.3.16 aged 31. Commemorated SGC Anglican Q1 9 and buried in I.I.18 Menin Road South Military Cemetery. Son of Frank and Rebecca Crossland of 80 William St, Sheffield; husband of the late Agnes Crossland. (see page 68)

Private **James Cumming** 292604 Gordon Highlanders 7ᵗʰ Bn. KIA 23.4.17 aged 28. Commemorated SGC Noncon DD 33 and Bay 8-9 Arras Memorial. Son of Robert and Christina Cumming.

Private **Sydney Darwent** 269059 Duke of Wellington's (West Riding Reg.) 1ˢᵗ/7ᵗʰ Bn. Died of wounds 22.11.1917 aged 19. Commemorated SGC Anglican K2 109 and buried XXVII. BB.6 Lijssenthoek Military Cemetery. Son of Eleanor Darwent of Sheffield and the late Mr Charles Darwent.

Midshipman **Bernard Walter Davy** Royal Naval Reserve. KIA 10.7.16 at Imbros aged 21. Commemorated SGC Noncon H 124 and buried in K 82 The Lancashire Landing Cemetery, Turkey. Son of Alfred South Davy and Lydia Davy of 31 Dover Rd, Sheffield. (see page 65)

Private **Fred Dawson** 14294 KOYLI 7th Bn. KIA 24.8.16 aged 24. Commemorated SGC Anglican J2 60 and Pier and Face 11C and 12A Thiepval Memorial. Brother of Harry Dawson of 121 Neill Rd, Sheffield.

Pioneer **Edwin Mossforth Doughty** 209630 Royal Engineers M Company No.3 Spec. Rly. Bn. KIA 1.3.17 aged 21. Commemorated SGC Noncon JJ 165 and buried IV.E.6 Ecoivres Military Cemetery, Mont-St.Eloi. (see page 70)

Second Lieutenant **Harold Edward Dyson** York and Lancs Regiment 4th (Hallamshire) Bn. (Territorial). KIA 31.7.16 aged 23. Commemorated SGC Anglican Z 51 and buried I.A.25 Blighty Valley Cemetery, Authuille Wood. Son of Henry and Hannah Dyson of 89 Cowlishaw Rd, Sheffield. (see page 66)

Lieutenant **John Norris Eaton** Canadian Infantry 43rd Bn. KIA 5.4.17 aged 21. Commemorated SGC Noncon AA 96 and buried V.B. 27 Ecoivres Military Cemetery Mont-St.Eloi. Son of Frank E and Mary G Eaton of England. (see page 71)

Private **James Cyril Eccleston** 202682 KOYLI 1st/4th Bn. Died of wounds (gas poisoning) 25.7.17 aged 20. Commemorated SGC Anglican C2 170 and buried II. K.2 Mont Huon Cemetery, Le Treport. Son of James and Annie Eccleston(e) of Sheffield. (see page 74)

Sergeant **William Farr** 12340 KOYLI 9th Bn. KIA 27.11.15 aged 26. Commemorated SGC Anglican Q 107 and buried in IX.D.49 Cite Bonjean Military Cemetery, Armentieres. Only son of Gertrude and the late William Farr.

Sergeant **George Forrest** 492 York and Lancs 4th Bn. Died 2.7.1916 aged 25. Buried SGC Anglican S1 73. Husband of Mary E. Forrest of 64 Clough Rd, Sheffield. (see page 19)

Lieutenant **Harold Brooke Forsdike** York and Lancs Regiment 14th Bn.

(2nd Barnsley Pals). KIA 1.7.16 aged 24. Commemorated SGC Anglican T1 179 and Pier and Face 14A and 14B Thiepval Memorial. Son of William and Emily Forsdike of Parkfield House, Norfolk Road, Sheffield. (see page 58)

Private **Edward Stanley Garwell** 34955 East Yorkshire Regiment C Coy 7th Bn. Died of wounds 21.9.18 aged 29. Commemorated SGC Anglican Z1 175 and buried VII.G.10A Mont Huon Military Cemetery, Le Treport. Son of Jesse and Emma Garwell of 71 Thirlwell Road, Heeley, Sheffield. (see page 81)

Private **Albert E. Gautier** 18672 York and Lancs 1st Bn. KIA 9.8.15 aged 17. Commemorated SGC Anglican R1 9 and buried in J 6 Kemmel Chateau Military Cemetery, Belgium. Son of Mrs E. Gautier of 34 Tapton Bank, Manchester Road, Sheffield and the late Sergeant F. H. Gautier. His father and brother also died on active service. (see page 57)

Sergeant **Francis Herbert Gautier** 10885 Cheshire Reg. 11th Bn. Died 11.6.1916 aged 44. Buried SGC Anglican R1 9. Husband of Edna Gautier, 34 Tapton Bank, Manchester Rd, Sheffield. (see page 23)

Private **Walter Louis Giddy** 242982 KOYLI 1st/5th Bn. KIA 9.10.17 aged 31. Commemorated SGC Anglican A2 62 and Panel 108-111 Tyne Cot Memorial. Son of William H. Giddy, husband of Florence M. Giddy of 4 Fenwood Place, Common Side, Sheffield. (see page 75)

Private **Albert Victor Giles** 38845 York and Lancs Regiment. KIA 12.4.18 aged 20. Commemorated SGC Anglican C3 173 and Panel 125 and 128 Tyne Cot Memorial. Only son of Frederick A. and Annie Giles of 126 Ranby Road, Greystones, Sheffield. (see page 80)

Second Lieutenant **Walter H. Grady** 20339 Royal Fusiliers 6th Bn. KIA 25.4.15 aged 28. Commemorated SGC Anglican E 60 and on Panel 6 and 8 of the Ypres (Menin Gate) Memorial. Son of the late Mr and Mrs W Grady of Sheffield; husband of Ida Grady of 26, Thorney Hedge Road, Gunnersbury, London. (see page 55)

Private **Thomas Cyril Guy** 203339 Yorkshire Regiment 5th Bn. KIA 27.5.18 aged 28. Commemorated SGC Anglican R1 45 and buried Plot 1 Row D

Grave 19 Acheux British Cemetery. Husband of Nora E. Guy of 8 Maria St, Seaham Harbour, County Durham. (see page 78)

Air Mechanic 1st Class **Fred Harrison** 44544 Royal Air Force 28th Wing (A.D.S.). Died 10.7.1918 aged 36. Buried SGC Anglican R1 143. Son of the late Joseph and Mary Ann Harrison; husband of Mary Ellen Harrison of 32 Earldom Rd., Sheffield. (see page 31)

Private **George Charles Hastings** 19063 York and Lancs Regiment 9th Bn. KIA 1.7.16 aged 25. Commemorated SGC Noncon OO 82 and buried V.H.3 Blighty Valley Cemetery, Authuille Wood. Husband of Mary Hastings of Sheffield. (see page 60)

Private **Peter Hibberd** 3/6545 East Yorkshire Reg 3rd Bn. Died 11.11.1914 aged 30. Buried SGC Anglican A2 126. (see page 17)

Private **George Hibberson** 201205 York and Lancs Regiment 'C' Coy 2/4th Hallamshire (TF) Bn. KIA 3.5.17 aged 38. Commemorated SGC Noncon KK95 and Bay 8, Arras Memorial. Son of George and Emma Hibberson, stepson of Ellen Hibberson of 389 Shoreham Street, Sheffield.

Private **George Hillman** G/29553 The Prince of Wales's Own (Middlesex Regiment). KIA 22.10.16 aged 32. Commemorated SGC Anglican B2 105 and Pier and Face 12D and 13B Thiepval Memorial. Son of George and Priscilla Hillman of 85 Peveril Road, Sheffield; husband of Florence Mary Hillman, 66 Castle Road, St Albans, Herts.

Sergeant **Ralph Leonard Hinde** 6310 Northamptonshire Regiment. KIA 5.5.15 aged 31. Commemorated SGC Anglican T1 116 and on Panel 28 to 30 Le Touret Memorial. Son of John and Lydia Hinde, Bedfordshire; husband of the late Annie Hinde, Sheffield. (see page 56)

Private **Alfred John Honer** 240974 Cameronians (Scottish Rifles) 56th Bn. KIA 14.4.17 aged 19. Commemorated SGC Anglican W 98 and Bay 6 Arras Memorial. Son of William and Elizabeth Honer of 18 Meadowbank Avenue, Sheffield. (see page 71)

Lieutenant **Douglas James Honer** Royal Flying Corps 55th Squadron and Royal Field Artillery. KIA 4.6.17 aged 23. Commemorated SGC Anglican W 98 and on the Arras Flying Memorial. Son of William and Elizabeth

Honer of 18 Meadowbank Avenue, Sheffield. (see page 71)

Private **Henry Hunter** 13247 East Yorkshire Regiment 11th Bn. KIA 12.4.18. Commemorated SGC Anglican H1 93 and Panel 4 Ploegsteert Memorial. Son of Dennis and Susan Hunter of 29 Bath Street, Sheffield. (see page 77)

Corporal **Jack Heathcote Hyder** 17647 Royal Sussex Regiment 9th Bn. KIA 22.3.18 aged 20. Commemorated SGC Anglican H3 60 and Marchelpot Brit. Cem. Mem. 90, Roye New British Cemetery. Son of William and Ada Hyder of Sussex, and grandson of Henry and Mary Heathcote.

Private **Albert Edward Jay** 27185 KOYLI 6th Bn. Died of wounds 21.9.16. Commemorated SGC Anglican I 1 44 and buried B 17 15 St Sever Cemetery, Rouen. Son of Charles and Grace Jay of 182 Pomona St, Ecclesall; husband of Nellie Jay, of 140 Pomona St, Ecclesall, Sheffield. (see page 68)

Gunner **Harold James Jinkinson** (Jenkinson) 606294 Royal Horse Artillery and Royal Field Artillery Territorial Force B Battery 296th Brigade. Died of wounds 29.9.17 aged 28. Commemorated SGC Anglican Z1 77 and buried VII. 1F 18 Dozinghem Military Cemetery. Son of Amos and Rosa Jinkinson.

Private **Ernest Johnson** 12715 KOYLI 7th Bn. Died of wounds 3.4.18 aged 35. Commemorated SGC Anglican M1 55 and buried I.K.16 Namps-au-val British Cemetery. Son of Edwin and Elizabeth Johnson of Sheffield. (Obituary says he died in casualty clearing station.)

Corporal **Frank Johnson** 24496 York and Lancs Regiment 12th Bn. KIA 27.6.17 aged 24. Commemorated SGC Anglican M2 17 and Bay 8 Arras Memorial. Son of the late George and Charlotte Johnson of 83 Riverdale Rd, Sheffield.

Private **Herbert Knapton** 38705 KOYLI C Company 9th Bn. KIA 22.3.18 aged 19. Commemorated SGC Anglican C1 125 and Panel 59 and 60 Pozieres Memorial. Son of George E. and Sophia C. Knapton of 5 Arley St, Sheffield.

Sapper **Arthur Thomas Lea** 259675 Royal Engineers 4th Sig. Corps. Died of TB 10.9.1918 aged 34. Buried SGC Noncon P 36. Husband of Alice Douglas Lea. (see page 33)

Private **John Lindop** 5799 York and Lancs Reg 3rd/4th Bn. Died of meningitis 31.12.1916 aged 29. Buried SGC Anglican R1 34. Son of the late Albert and Sarah Lindop, husband of Florence Wells (formerly Lindop) of 17 Wreakin Place, Carbrook, Sheffield. (see page 25)

Driver **William Linley** (not on the CWGC website) T2/125 Army Service Corps. Died of lympho sarcoma and heart failure 5.1.1918. Buried SGC Noncon JJ162. Son of Samuel and Mary Linley. (see page 29)

Lance Corporal **Henry Pearson Lister** 45388 Durham Light Infantry 2nd Bn. KIA 23.10.18 aged 19. Commemorated SGC Anglican T2 49 and buried I.A.36 St. Souplet British Cemetery. Son of Mr and Mrs H. L. Lister of 44 Ball Rd, Hillsborough, Sheffield.

Corporal **Charles Henry Littlehales** 2115 (Hallamshire) Bn. York and Lancs. Died 2.11.1918 aged 24. Buried SGC Anglican T1 108. Husband of Emma Littlehales, 34 Moore St, Sheffield. (see page 37)

Captain **Stewart Maleham** York and Lancs Regiment 13th Bn. KIA 1.7.16 aged 37. Commemorated SGC Anglican U1 33 and buried C 34, Queens Cemetery, Puisieux. Son of Henry and Elizabeth Maleham of 15 Endcliffe Avenue, Sheffield.

Sergeant **William Horace Mann** CH/13136 Royal Marine Light Infantry. Lost at sea 22.9.14 aged 29. Commemorated SGC Anglican G1 187 and Chatham Naval Memorial. Son of Charles and Jane Mann, 575 Abbeydale Road, Sheffield; husband of J.U. Mann of 121 Hope St, Sheerness, Kent. (see page 53)

Private **Graham Mannifield** 30231 KOYLI 2nd/5th Bn. KIA 1.2.18 aged 30. Commemorated SGC Anglican A3 81 and buried III.F.26 Roclincourt Military Cemetery. Son of Ernest and Mary Mannifield; husband of Ethel Mannifield of 23 Cockayne Place, Meersbrook, Sheffield. (see page 76)

Private **John Arthur Marriott** 18384 Labour Corps. Died 6.3.1919 aged 25. Buried SGC Anglican H1 159. Son of George and Clara Marriott, 49 Court, 3 House, Pearl St, Sheffield; husband of Mrs Greenhedge (formerly

Marriott), 15 Summerfield St, Sheffield. (see page 45)

2nd Corporal **Edwin Marsden** 17502 Royal Engineers 17th Field Company. KIA 23.8.14 aged 27. Commemorated SGC Anglican F 56 and buried I.D.12 Hautrage Military Cemetery. Son of Arthur and Sarah Marsden of 'Stanmore', Heatherfield, Totley, Sheffield. (see page 51)

Gunner **Albert Abel Martin** 54752 Royal Horse Artillery and Royal Field Artillery 6th Ammunition Column. Died a prisoner of war 5.10.16 aged 26. Commemorated SGC Anglican L2 69 and Baghdad (North Gate) War Cemetery. His older brother was killed in France. Son of James and Rosina Martin. (see page 67)

Private **Henry Martin** 18484 York and Lancs Regiment 8th Bn. Died of wounds 16.9.16 aged 37. Commemorated SGC Anglican L2 69 and buried I.B.18 Contalmaison Chateau Cemetery. Son of James and Rosina Martin; husband of Ada A. Martin of 18 Norton Lees Rd, Meersbrook, Sheffield. (see page 67)

Captain **William Stanley Meeke** The Duke of Cambridge's Own Middlesex Regiment 2nd Bn. KIA 1.7.16 aged 28. Commemorated SGC Noncon HH 101 and buried XV.1.3 Ovillers Military Cemetery. Son of the late Joseph and Mary Meeke of Sheffield. Military Cross. (see page 60)

Private **Tom Moseley** DM2/223832 Army Service Corps. Died of bronchitis 20.1.1917 aged 27. Buried SGC Anglican S1 50. (see page 26)

Second Lieutenant **Maurice Nicholson** Royal Flying Corps 11th Squadron and General List Army Cyclist Corps. KIA 18.8.17 aged 30. Commemorated SGC Noncon N 84 and Arras Flying Services Memorial. Son of Arthur J. and Mary Ann Nicholson of Sheffield. (see page 75)

Lance Corporal **William Nield** 6454 Duke of Cambridge's Own 17th Lancers. KIA 29.10.14 aged 32. Commemorated SGC Anglican D3 173 and Panel 5 Ypres (Menin Gate) Memorial. Son of the late Walter and Mary Ann Nield; brother of Kate Nield of 599 Abbeydale Rd, Sheffield.

Private **Harold Norris** 12/199 York and Lancs Regiment 12th Bn. KIA 1.7.16 aged 26. Commemorated SGC Noncon W 176 and buried D 13, Railway Hollow Cemetery, Hebuterne. Son of James and Sarah H. Norris of 11 Ward Place, Highfield, Sheffield. His brother was also KIA. (see page 60)

Private **Rowland Norris** 38410 King's Own (Royal Lancaster Regiment) 9th Bn. formerly Royal Army Medical Corps. KIA Salonika 19.9.18 aged 21. Commemorated SGC Noncon W 176 and the Doiran Memorial, Greece. Son of James and Sarah H. Norris of 11 Ward Place, Highfield, Sheffield. (see page 60)

Air Mechanic 3rd Class **Frank Osguthorpe** 136360 Royal Air Force. Accidently killed whilst swinging a propellor 25.8.1918 aged 19. Buried SGC Anglican Z 73. (see page 31)

Private **William James Osguthorpe** 264284 Labour Corps. Died of TB 20.8.1920 aged 25. Buried SGC Anglican Z 73. (see page 31)

Second Lieutenant **Albert Edgar Palmer** The Prince of Wales's Own (West Yorkshire Regiment) 8th Bn. KIA 27.9.18 aged 26. Commemorated SGC Anglican R1 27 Con and buried I.D.2 Flesquieres Hill British Cemetery. Son of T.E. Palmer, of Wath Road, Sheffield; husband of Clara Palmer of South View, Grimethorpe, Yorkshire.

Private **Walter Andrews Parke** 16927 Welsh Reg. Died 20.5.1919 aged 47. Buried SGC Anglican X2 102. (see page 46)

Private **Charles Herbert Parkin** 19418 KOYLI 10th Bn. KIA 1.7.16 aged 20. Commemorated SGC Anglican M1 135 and Pier and Face 11C and 12A Thiepval Memorial. Son of Amy Parkin of 52 William St, Sheffield and the late Charles Parkin.

Private **Thomas Robert Peck** 203579 York and Lancs . Died of wounds 13.11.1919 aged 40. Buried SGC Anglican N 13. Husband of Edna Peck. (see page 48)

Private **Joseph William Stanley Pickering** 405368 Royal Army Medical Corps. Died 20.11.1918 aged 20. Buried SGC Anglican B1 79. (see page 42)

2nd Lieutenant **Wilfred Downes Pollard** Notts & Derby (Sherwood Foresters) 15th Bn. Died of wounds 26.4.1918 aged 24. Buried SGC Anglican E1 38. (see page 30)

Private **William Redfearn** 65831 Machine Gun Corps Infantry Bn. Died of wounds 22.5.18 aged 23. Commemorated SGC Noncon BB 54 and buried V.J.5A Mont Huon Military Cemetery, Le Treport. Son of George and Mary Redfearn, 169 Ecclesall Road, Sheffield. (see page 78)

2nd Lieutenant **Albert Henry Rodgers** Royal Field Artillery 4th (Reserve) Brigade. Died in hospital 7.11.18 aged 29. Buried SGC Noncon O 124. (see page 40)

Private **Branson Saltfleet** 60097 York and Lancs Regiment 2nd Bn. Died of wounds 18.10.18 aged 28. Commemorated SGC Anglican A3 13 and buried II.C.6 Vadencourt British Cemetery, Maissemy. Husband of Lily Saltfleet, 12 Court 2 House, Broomhall St, Sheffield. (see page 79)

Private **Roger Sellers** (Sellars) 17179 York and Lancs Regiment 8th Bn. KIA 1.7.16 aged 32. Commemorated SGC Anglican S1 109 and Pier and Face 14A and 14B Thiepval Memorial. Husband of Beatrice Sellers, 47 Lansdowne Road, Sheffield.

Private **Edward Shemeld** 1653 York and Lancs / 25023 Machine Gun Corps (Infantry) 31st Company. KIA 30.3.18 aged 29. Commemorated SGC Anglican K19 and Bay 10 Arras Memorial. Son of Mr and Mrs Shemeld of 32 Hill St, Sheffield. Husband of May Slingsby (formerly Shemeld) of 12 Calvert Rd, Darnall, Sheffield. (see page 77)

Second Lieutenant **Ernest Ronald Shuttleworth** LZ/987 Royal Warwickshire Regiment. KIA 1.7.16 aged 22. Commemorated SGC Anglican H 37 and on Pier and Face 9A, 9B and 10B Thiepval Memorial. Son of Thomas E. and Mary E. Shuttleworth of 5 Park Avenue, Riverdale Rd, Sheffield. (see page 63)

Private **Albert Ernest Smith** 43065 The Prince of Wales's Own (West Yorkshire Regiment) 11th Bn. KIA 7.6.17 aged 27. Commemorated SGC Noncon O 127 and on Panel 21 of Ypres (Menin Gate) Memorial. Son of George and Emma C. Smith, 45 Sherrington Road, Sheffield. (see page 73)

Private **Charles Hartley Smith** 10934 Royal Fusiliers 23rd Bn. Died of wounds 21.10.16 aged 22. Commemorated SGC Anglican J 167 and buried II.B.10 Couin British Cemetery. Son of John Hartley and Sarah Ann Smith of 25 Endcliffe Avenue, Endcliffe Crescent, Sheffield.

Private **Fred Parker Smith** 12/1056 York and Lancs Regiment 12th Bn. Died of wounds 4.7.16 aged 21. Commemorated SGC Anglican B1 112 and buried IV.B.20 Doullens Communal Cemetery Extension No.1. Son of Clara and the late Charles Henry Smith of Sheffield.

Private **George William Smith** 25897 York and Lancs Regiment 14th Bn. Died of wounds 31.5.17 aged 29. Commemorated SGC Noncon O 127 and buried in XXV F 13 Etaples Military Cemetery. Husband of Alice Smith, 20 Grosvenor Square, Sheffield; son of George and Emma C. Smith, 45 Sherrington Road, Sheffield. (see page 73)

Rifleman **Charles Southern** 20335 Royal Irish Rifles, 15th Bn. KIA 20.10.18 aged 23. Commemorated SGC Anglican E1 70 and buried VIII.D.16 Harlebeke New British Cemetery. Son of Charles H. and Annie Southern of 244 Queens Road, Sheffield.

Private **Leonard Staley** 268848 Duke of Wellington's (West Riding) Regiment, 2nd/6th Bn. KIA 27.11.17 aged 30. Commemorated SGC Anglican A2 153 and Panel 6 and 7 Cambrai Memorial, Louverval. Son of William and Mary Staley of Sheffield. Wife Edith predeceased him. (see page 76)

Lance Corporal **Harold Steeples** 10218 KOYLI 3rd Battalion. Died in hospital 11.4.16 aged 26. Buried SGC Anglican K3 112. (see page 18)

Captain **Albert Charles Stevens** Royal Engineers. Died 21.5.1917 aged 55. Buried SGC Anglican Y 108. (see page 28)

Driver **Herbert Stuart** 83658 Royal Field Artillery. Died 1.6.1919 aged 21. Buried SGC Anglican R1 183. (see page 47)

Lance Corporal **Arthur Henry Thomas** 16374 KOYLI 8th Bn. KIA 1.7.16 age 29. Commemorated SGC Anglican S1 12 and Pier and Face 11C and 12A Thiepval Memorial. Son of Arthur G. and Elizabeth Thomas of 7 Winter St, Sheffield.

Captain **Duncan Collison Willey Thomas** Argyle and Sutherland Highlanders 4th Bn attd Gordon Highlanders. KIA 12.11.14 aged 23. Commemorated SGC Anglican H 147 and Panel 42 and 44 Ypres (Menin

Gate) Memorial. Son of Lt. Col. W.F. Thomas and Jane Thomas of 'Dunmere', 17 Eaton Rd, Branksome Park, Bournemouth.

Signaller **Arthur Thompson** Z/6967 Royal Naval Volunteer Reserve. Died 17.12.1918 aged 20. Buried SGC Anglican Y1 164. (see page 43)

2ⁿᵈ Lieutenant **Robert Saxelby Vine** Cambridgeshire Reg 1ˢᵗ Bn. KIA 14.10.16 aged 25. Commemorated SGC Noncon II 2 and Pier and Face 16B Thiepval Memorial. Only son of G.R. and Alice Vine of Totley, Sheffield; husband of Elsie Vine.

Corporal **John Herbert Wain** 10962 Army Cyclist Corps 8ᵗʰ Cyclist Bn. KIA 8.6.18 aged 27. Commemorated SGC Anglican K1 73 and on Spanish Memorial near North West entrance Vandieres (or Vandieres-sous-Chatillon) churchyard. Son of Josiah and A.A. Wain of 17 South Grove Rd, Sheffield.

Private **Joseph Wainwright** 3046 Royal Army Medical Corps. Died 6.5.1916 aged 30. Buried SGC Anglican L3 112. (see page 18)

Second Lieutenant **Charles Henry Wardill** Yorks and Lancs Regiment 15ᵗʰ Bn attd 12ᵗʰ Bn. KIA 1.7.16 aged 39. Commemorated SGC Noncon KK 118 and Pier and Face 14A and 14B Thiepval Memorial. Son of James and Eliza Wardill, Sheffield; husband of Edith E. Wardill of 8 Violet Bank Rd, Nether Edge, Sheffield. Brother Sydney also died. (see page 65)

Rifleman **Robert Watson** R/18976 Kings Royal Rifle Corps 1ˢᵗ Bn. KIA 17.2.17 aged 22. Commemorated SGC Anglican Q1 114 and buried IV.F.15 Regina Trench Cemetery, Grandcourt. Son of Robert C (late) and Sarah Sophia Watson of Sheffield.

Lance Corporal **Henry William Wharton** 12/264 York and Lancs 12ᵗʰ Bn. KIA 1.7.16 aged 20. Commemorated SGC Anglican D1 158 and buried C 19 Queens Cemetery, Puisieux. Son of William and Charlotte Wharton of 84 Sandford Grove Rd, Nether Edge, Sheffield.

Private **Arthur White** 8157 Coldstream Guards 2ⁿᵈ Bn. KIA 5.11.14 aged 27. Commemorated SGC Anglican D 50 and buried IV.J.8 Sanctuary Wood Cemetery. Son of Jim and Lydia White of Fawcett St, Sheffield; husband of Gertrude Smith (formerly White) of 66 Wayland Rd, Sharrow, Sheffield.

Lieutenant **Laurence Whiteley** Black Watch (Royal Highlanders) 5th (Angus and Dundee) Bn. KIA 31.7.17 aged 32. Commemorated SGC Anglican U1 43 and on Spanish Memorial A4 Wieltje Farm Cemetery. Son of Seth and Annie E. Whiteley, 30 Collegiate Crescent, Sheffield. (see page 74)

Private **Thomas Whiting** 3/1754 KOYLI. Died 28.11.1916 aged 37. Buried SGC Anglican H2 149. (see page 24)

Lance Corporal **Noel Wilcock** 12/1097 York and Lancs Regiment 12th Bn. KIA 1.7.16 aged 23. Commemorated SGC Anglican F 53 and buried D 54 Queens Cemetery Puisieux. Son of Mr and Mrs J.T. Wilcock of 5 Priory Rd, Sharrow, Sheffield.

Private **Fred Williams** 36609 Northumberland Fusilliers 11th Bn. KIA 6.7.17 aged 22. Commemorated SGC Anglican H1 68 and Panel 8 and 12 Ypres (Menin Gate) Memorial. Son of Mr T. and Mrs M. E. Williams of Sheffield.

Private **Harry Wilson** 50021 Highland Light Infantry. Died 30.7.1919 aged 20. Buried SGC Anglican G1 18. (see page 48)

Private **Cyril Woodhead** 36062 East Surrey Regiment posted to 1st/21st Bn London Regiment (First Surrey Rifles). Died of wounds 7.1.18 aged 31. Commemorated SGC Anglican Q1 115 and buried IX.F.9 Rocquigny-Equancourt Road British Cemetery, Manancourt. Son of Thomas and Annie Woodhead; husband of Winifred Woodhead of 12 Talbot Place, The Park, Sheffield.

Ordinary Seaman **William Spender Yates** Tyneside Z/13005 Royal Naval Volunteer Reserve. Died 8.10.1918 aged 18. Buried SGC Anglican N1 147. (see page 37)

Abbreviations used in the text

CWGC - Commonwealth War Graves Commission

KIA - Killed in action

KOYLI - King's Own Yorkshire Light Infantry

MI - Memorial Inscription

SGC - Sheffield General Cemetery

SGC Anglican - the consecrated area of the Cemetery

SGC Noncon - the Nonconformist area of the Cemetery

York and Lancs – the York and Lancaster Regiment

Sources

Sheffield General Cemetery Trust database (www.gencem.org)

Commonwealth War Graves Commission (www.cwgc.org)

Sheffield Archives and Local Studies Library
(www.sheffield.gov.uk/libraries)

Forces War Records (www.forces-war-records.co.uk)

www.Ancestry.co.uk

www.findmypast.co.uk

National Archives (www.nationalarchives.gov.uk)

British Newspaper Archive (www.britishnewspaperarchive.co.uk)

Imperial War Museum (www.iwm.org.uk)

National Army Museum (www.nam.ac.uk)

York and Lancaster Regimental Museum (www.cliftonpark.org.uk)

Sheffield University Library (www.sheffield.ac.uk)

Bibliography

The Great War Handbook - A guide for family historians and students of the conflict. Geoff Bridger. Pen and Sword Books 2009.

Sheffield cares for the wounded. Dr. Derek R. Cullen Editor. J. W. Northend Ltd 2014.

The Home Front - Sheffield in the First World War. Scott Lomax. Pen and Sword Books 2014.

Sheffield City Battalion - The 12th (Service) Battalion York and Lancaster Regiment. Ralph Gibson and Paul Oldfield. Pen and Sword Books 2010.

Sheffield in the Great War. Peter Warr. Pen and Sword Books 2015.

The First World War. A J P Taylor. Penguin 1963.

A History of Sheffield. David Hey. Carnegie Publishing 1998.

A Testament of Youth. Vera Brittain. Virago 2014.

Diary of a Nursing Sister. Anon. Amberley Publishing 2014.

Not Forgotten. Neil Oliver. Hodder and Stoughton 2005.

Wounded - From Battlefield to Blighty. Emily Mayhew. Bodley Head 2013.

The World War One Source Book. Philip J. Haythornthwaite. Arms and Armour Press 1992.

Great Britain's Great War. Jeremy Paxman. Penguin 2013.

Love Tommy, Letters Home from the Great War to the Present Day. Andrew Roberts. Osprey Publishing 2012.

"A life too soon done" is one of a series of books created by volunteers of the Sheffield General Cemetery Trust which can be purchased through our website at **www.gencem.org**

Remote and Undisturbed

An illustrated history of the General Cemetery from its beginnings in 1836, to provide much needed burial space for a rapidly growing city, through to the present day.

£7.95

Danger and Despair

A fascinating picture of Victorian life through the vivid descriptions of untimely death. Drawn from the Cemetery's burial records, these are tales of tragic accidents, rejected love, deep despair and sometimes plain foolishness.

£7.95

Dead Good

A beautifully illustrated children's history book (ideal for 8 - 12 years) which gives a glimpse into the lives of children and people in Victorian Sheffield who are buried in the General Cemetery. Some experiences are funny, some scary and some very sad.

£4.95

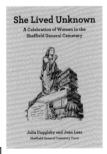

She Lived Unknown

This booklet is a celebration of the lives of women buried in the General Cemetery focusing on poverty, the history of nursing and the way women are symbolised in the Cemetery.

£2.95